Microwave
CHINESE COOKING

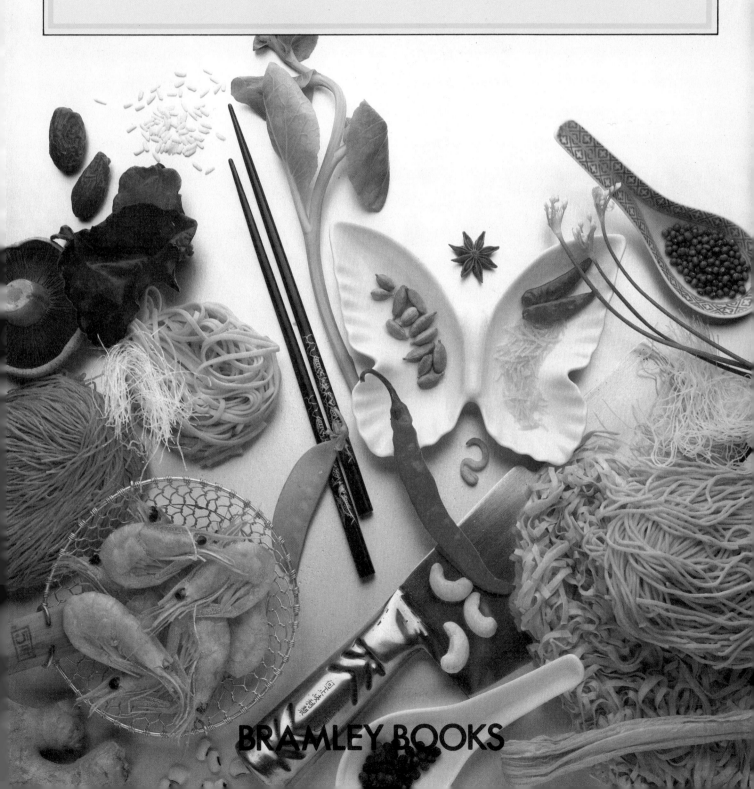

BRAMLEY BOOKS

Compiled by Judith Ferguson
Tested and Prepared by Jacqueline Bellefontaine
Photographed by Peter Barry
Designed by Sara Cooper
Produced by Ted Smart, Gerald Hughes and David Gibbon

CLB 1740
Published 1986 by Bramley Books, Godalming, Surrey.
© 1986 Illustrations and Text: Colour Library Books Ltd.,
    Guildford, Surrey, England.
Text filmsetting by Focus Photoset, London, England.
Printed and bound in Barcelona, Spain by Cronion S.A.
ISBN 0 86283 494 5

**Microwave oven used for testing and preparation for
  photography, supplied by Samsung Electronics (UK) Ltd.**

CONTENTS

GENERAL INTRODUCTION

People are usually of two minds about microwave ovens. Experienced cooks are sceptical. Inexperienced cooks are mystified. Most people who don't own one think a microwave oven is an expensive luxury. Those of us who have one, though, would find it difficult to give it up. Great advances have been made in the design and capabilities of microwave ovens since the demand for them first began in the Sixties. With so many kinds of ovens available, both beginners and advanced cooks can find one that best suits their particular needs.

How Microwave Ovens Work

Microwave ovens, whatever the make or model, do have certain things in common. The energy that makes fast cooking possible is comprised of electromagnetic waves converted from electricity. Microwaves are a type of high frequency radio wave. The waves are of short length, hence the name microwave.

Inside the oven is a magnetron, which converts ordinary electricity into microwaves. A wave guide channels the microwaves into the oven cavity, and a stirrer fan circulates them evenly. Microwaves are attracted to the particles of moisture that form part of any food. As the microwaves are absorbed, to a depth of about 4-5cm/1¹/₂-2 inches, they cause the water molecules in the food to vibrate, about 2000 million times a second. This generates the heat that cooks the food. The heat reaches the centre of the food by conduction, just as in ordinary cooking. However, this is accomplished much faster than in conventional cooking because no heat is generated until

the waves are absorbed by the food. All the energy is concentrated on cooking the food and not on heating the oven itself or the baking dishes. Standing time is often necessary to allow the food to continue cooking after it is removed from the oven.

Most microwave ovens have an ON indicator light and a timer control. Some timer controls look like minute timers, while others are calibrated in seconds up to 50 seconds and minutes up to 30 minutes. This can vary slightly; some models have a 10 minute interval setting. Some ovens have a separate ON-OFF switch, while others switch on with the timer or power setting. Almost all have a bell or buzzer to signal the end of cooking time.

Microwave Oven Features

At this point, things really begin to diversify. Different terms are used for the same power setting depending on what brand of oven you buy. Some ovens have a wider range of different settings as well. Chart No. 1 on power settings reconciles most of the popular terms.

Some ovens come equipped with a temperature probe which allows you to cook food according to its internal temperature instead of by time. It is most useful for roasting large cuts of meat. The probe needle is inserted into the thickest part of the food and the correct temperature set on the attached control. When that internal temperature is reached, the oven automatically turns off, or switches to a low setting to keep the food warm. Special microwave thermometers are also available to test internal temperature and can be used inside the oven. Conventional thermometers must never be used inside a microwave oven, but can be used outside.

A cooking guide is a feature on some ovens, either integrated into the control panel or on the top or side of the oven housing. It is really a summary of the information found in the instruction and recipe booklet that accompanies every oven. However, it does act as a quick reference and so can be a time saver.

CHART 1 Power Setting Comparison Chart

	Other Terms and Wattages	Uses
Low	ONE or TWO, KEEP WARM, 25%, SIMMER, DEFROST. 75-300 watts.	Keeping food warm. Softening butter, cream cheese and chocolate. Heating liquid to dissolve yeast. Gentle cooking.
Medium	THREE or FOUR, 50%, STEW, BRAISE, ROAST, REHEAT, MEDIUM-LOW, FIVE, 40%, MEDIUM-HIGH, SIX, 60-75%.. 400-500 watts.	Roasting meat and poultry. Stewing and braising less tender cuts of meat. Baking cakes and custards. Cooking hollandaise sauces.
High	SEVEN, FULL, ROAST, BAKE, NORMAL, 100%.	Quick cooking. Meats, fish, vegetables, biscuits/cookies, pasta, rice, breads, pastry, desserts.

Turntables eliminate the need for rotating baking dishes during cooking, although when using a square or loaf dish you may need to change its position from time to time anyway. Turntables are usually glass or ceramic and can be removed for easy cleaning. Of all the special features available, turntables are one of the most useful.

Certain ovens have one or more shelves so that several dishes can be accommodated at once. Microwave energy is higher at the top of the oven than on the floor and the more you cook at once the longer it all takes. However, these ovens accommodate larger baking dishes than those with turntables.

If you do a lot of entertaining, then an oven with a keep warm setting is a good choice. These ovens have a very low power setting that can keep food warm without further cooking for up to one hour. If you want to programme your oven like a computer, choose one with a memory control that can switch settings automatically during the cooking cycle.

Browning elements are now available built into microwave ovens. They look and operate much the same as conventional electric grills. If you already have a grill, you probably don't need a browning element. Some of the most recent ovens allow the browning element to be used at the same time as the microwave setting, which is a plus.

Combination ovens seem to be the answer to the problem of browning in a microwave oven. While the power settings go by different names in different models, generally there is a setting for microwave cooking alone, a convection setting with conventional electric heat and a setting which combines the two for almost the speed of microwave cooking with the browning ability of convection heat. However, the wattage is usually lower than in standard microwave ovens, and so cooking time will be slightly longer.

On combination settings, use recipes developed for microwave ovens, but follow the instructions with your particular oven for times and settings. Some ovens have various temperature settings to choose from. Breads, poultry, meat and pastries brown beautifully in these ovens, and conventional baking dishes, even metal, can be used with a special insulating mat. Beware of certain plastics though, as they can melt in a combination oven.

You can have your microwave oven built into the same unit as your conventional oven. Microwave ovens are best situated at eye level. In fact, there are now units available with gas or electric cooktops and a microwave oven underneath where the conventional oven used to be.

Safety and Cleaning

One of the questions most commonly asked is "Are microwave ovens safe to use?" They are safe because they have safety features built into them and they go through rigorous tests by their manufacturers and by independent agencies.

If you look at a number of microwave ovens you will see that the majority of them are lined with metal, and metal will not allow microwaves to pass through. The doors have special seals to keep the microwaves inside the oven and have cut-out devices to cut off microwave energy immediately the door is opened. There are no pans to upset, no open flames or hot elements and the interior of the oven stays cool enough to touch. Although microwave ovens don't heat baking dishes, the heat generated by the cooking food does, so it is a good idea to use oven gloves or pot holders to remove dishes from the oven. It is wise periodically to check the door of your oven to make sure it has not been bent. Check latches and hinges, too, to make sure they are in good working order. Don't use baking dishes that are too large to allow the turntable to rotate freely; this can cause the motor to over-heat or cause dents in the oven sides and door, lowering efficiency and affecting safety of operation.

Microwave ovens are cleaner and more hygienic to cook with than conventional gas and electric ovens. Foods do not spatter as much and spills do not burn, so clean-up is faster. The turntables and shelves can be removed for easier cleaning. Use non-abrasive cleansers and scrubbers, and be sure to wipe up

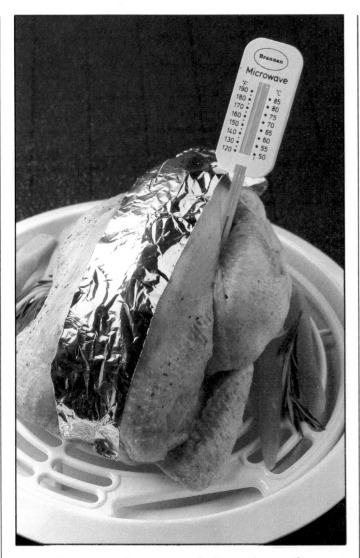

A special microwave thermometer, which is used to test the internal temperature of the food, can be used inside the oven.

any residue so that it does not build up around the door seals. Faster cooking times and lower electricity consumption combine to make microwave ovens cheaper to run, especially for cooking small amounts of food, than conventional ovens.

Once you have chosen your oven and understand what makes it work, the fun of cooking begins. There are some basic rules to remember, however, as with conventional cooking, but most of them are common sense.

Quantity

Food quantities affect cooking times. For example, one baked potato will take about 3-4 minutes, two will take about 6-7 minutes, four will take 10-11 minutes. Generally, if you double the quantity of a recipe, you need to increase the cooking time by about half as much again.

Density and Shape

The denser the food, the longer the cooking time. A large piece of meat is bound to take longer to cook than something light and porous like a cake or a loaf of bread. When cooking foods of various densities or shapes at the same time, special arrangements are necessary. For instance, place the thicker part of the food to the outside of the dish, thinner part toward the middle. Arrange pieces of food in a circle whenever possible, and in a round dish. If neither of these arrangements is possible, cover the thinner or less dense part of the food with foil for part of the cooking time. Rearrange and turn over such foods as asparagus or broccoli spears several times during cooking if they will not fit into your round dishes without considerable trimming.

Size

The smaller a piece of food the quicker it will cook. Pieces of food of the same kind and size will cook at the same rate. Add smaller or faster-cooking foods further along in the cooking time, such as mushrooms to a stew. If you have a choice of cooking heights, put food that is larger and can take more heat above food that is smaller and more delicate.

Covering

Most foods will cook, reheat or defrost better when covered. Use special covers that come with your cookware or simple cover with cling film. This covering must be pierced to release steam, otherwise it can balloon and possibly burst. Tight covering can give meat and poultry a "steamed" taste. Greaseproof paper or paper towels can also be used to keep in the heat and increase cooking efficiency.

Sugar or Fat Content

High sugar or fat content in certain foods means they will absorb microwave energy faster and reach a higher temperature. It is wise to cover food that will spatter, such as bacon, and to protect cakes that have very sugary toppings.

Standing Time

Microwave recipes usually advise leaving food to stand for 5-10 minutes after removal from the oven. Slightly undercooking the food allows the residual heat to finish it off, and microwave recipes take this into consideration. Meat and baked potatoes are usually wrapped in foil to contain the heat. Standing time also makes meat easier to carve. Cakes, breads and pastries should be left on a flat surface for their standing time as this helps to cook their bases. In general, foods benefit from being covered during standing time.

Above and left: the number and variety of different baking dishes and the range of equipment for the microwave is vast.

Equipment and Cookware

The number of different baking dishes and the range of equipment for microwave cooking is vast. There are so many highly specialised dishes for specific needs that to list them all would take up almost the whole of this book!

Explore cookware departments and find your own favourites. Follow your oven instruction booklet carefully since it will give you good advice on which cookware is best for your particular oven. Some dishes, lightweight plastics and even some hard plastics can't be used on combination settings. The temperature is too high and the dishes will melt or break. Most metal cookware can be used successfully in combination ovens, following the manufacturers guidelines. I have had less than satisfactory results with certain aluminium pans in my combination oven, so experimentation is essential. Paper bags can catch fire on High settings, and I have had the same experience with silicone-coated paper, although its use is often recommended. Microwave energy penetrates round shapes particularly efficiently, so round dishes and ring moulds work very well. The turntable can also be cooked on directly for such foods as scones or meringues or used for reheating foods like bread or coffee cakes.

For foods that are likely to boil over, like jams and soups, use the largest, deepest bowl that will fit into the oven cavity. Whole fish can be cooked in a cooking bag and curved to fit the shape of the turntable if they are too large to lie flat.

Browning dishes do work and the results are impressive. There are different designs and some have lids so that meat can be browned and finished off as a braise or stew in the same dish. Covering foods like chops or nut cutlets also speeds up the browning process. These dishes need to be preheated for between 4 to 8 minutes, depending on manufacturers instructions, and will get extremely hot. Use oven gloves or pot holders to remove browning dishes from the oven and set them on a heatproof mat to protect work surfaces. Butter will brown very fast, and steaks and chops can be seared. Stir frying is possible in a microwave oven with the use of a browning tray, and sausages brown beautifully without the shrinkage of conventional grilling or frying. These dishes can also be useful for browning a flour and fat roux for making sauces and gravies.

Cooking Poultry, Meat and Game

Moisture evaporates less readily during microwave cooking, so meat does not dry out. The fat in poultry will turn brown during cooking, but only in whole birds. Single joints of chicken or other poultry cook too quickly for the fat to brown. A thin layer of fat left on pork or beef for roasting will also brown, although it will not crisp. Fat is important to help keep the meat moist, but if you prefer to take it off, do so after cooking, or remember to baste frequently and cover the meat. There are a number of bastes, coatings and seasonings, some especially developed for microwave cooking, that can be used to give an appetizing brownness to meat and poultry.

Choose boned and rolled joints and cuts of meat that are a uniform thickness and shape. If this isn't possible, the next best thing is covering the thinner parts with foil for part of the cooking time. This trick with foil is also useful on poultry to cover the leg ends and the meat along the length of the breast bone. For poultry joints, cover the thinner ends of the breasts and the drumsticks.

Less tender cuts of meat, such as those for stewing, need to be cooked on a medium setting after initial browning. High settings can toughen these cuts of meat. Whether or not to salt

meat before cooking depends on which book you read. I think the general rules that apply to conventional meat cooking apply to microwave cooking as well. Do not salt meat to be roasted until after cooking. Sprinkle salt inside the cavity of poultry, if desired, and lightly salt stews and braises once the liquid has been added. Charts No. 2 and 3 serve as a quick reference, for meat, poultry and game.

Cooking Fish and Shellfish

The microwave oven excels at cooking fish. You can poach fish fillets in minutes. Arrange them in a dish in a circle with the thicker part of the fillet to the outside of the dish. If preparing a sauce to go with the fish, poach in a little white wine or water and lemon juice for a little more liquid to work with. A bay leaf, slice of onion and a few peppercorns are classic additions to the poaching liquid for extra flavour.

CHART 2 Meat, Poultry and Game (per 450g/1lb.)

	Mins. on High	Mins. on Medium	Internal Temperature Before Standing	After Standing
Beef: boned and rolled				
rare	6-7	11-13	57°C/130°F	62°C/140°F
medium	7-8	13-15	65°C/150°F	70°C/160°F
well-done	8-9	15-17	70°C/160°F	78°C/170°F
Beef: bone in				
rare	5	10	57°C/130°F	62°C/140°F
medium	6	11	65°C/150°F	70°C/160°F
well-done	8	15	70°C/160°F	78°C/170°F
Leg of Lamb	8-10	11-13	78°C/170°F	82°C/180°F
Veal	8-9	11-12	70°C/160°F	78°C/170°F
Pork	9-11	13-15	82°C/180°F	85°C/185°F
Ham				
Uncooked, boned	1st 5	15-18	55°C/130°F	70°C/160°F
Bone in	1st 5	15½-18½	55°C/130°F	70°C/160°F
Pre-cooked, boned	1st 5	12-15	55°C/130°F	
Bone in	1st 5	10-15		
Chicken	6-8	9-11	85°C/185°F	94°C/190°F
Duck	6-8	9-11	85°C/185°F	94°C/190°F
Turkey	9-11	12-15	85°C/185°F	94°C/190°F
Pheasant		20 total		
Poussins	15-20 total			
Wild Duck	5	10 total		
Pigeon	10 total			
Quail	5-9 total			

CHART 3 Small Cuts of Meat, Poultry and Game

Type	Mins. on High	Mins. on Medium	Special Instructions
Steaks (3.75mm/1½″ thick) 120g-180g/4-6oz			Use a browning dish pre-heated to manufacturer's instructions. Use timing for rare when cooking kebabs.
rare	2-3		
medium rare	3-4		
medium	5-7		
well-done	7-9		
Lamb Chops	7-9		Use a browning dish
		13-15	Cook in liquid
Lamb Fillet		10-12	Brown, then cook in liquid
Pork Chops	7-9		Use a browning dish
		13-15	Cook in liquid
Pork Fillet		15	Brown, then cook in liquid
Veal Chops	7-9		Use a browning dish
		13-15	Cook in liquid
Smoked Pork Chops	4-6		Pre-cooked and browned
Ham Steaks	3		Pre-cooked and browned
Minced/Ground Meat (450g/1lb)	5		Break up with a fork as it cooks
Hamburgers	2½-3		Use browning dish
Lamb Patties	2½-3		Use browning dish
Meatballs (675g/1½ lbs)	10-12		
Duck Portions			Use browning dish
1 Breast (boned)	6		
2 Legs		15	Brown each side first
Chicken			
1 Breast	2-3		Brown first if desired
1 Leg	3-4		
2 Pieces	3-6		
3 Pieces	4-7		
4 Pieces	7-9		
Turkey Escalopes/Cutlets	10-15		
Turkey Legs (450g/1lb)	1st 10	13-16	
Bacon		4	On rack or paper towels
		1	Per side on pre-heated browning dish
Sausages		2	Use browning dish

CHART 4 Fish and Shellfish (per 450g/1lb.)

Type	Mins. on high	Type	Mins. on high
Cod Steaks and Fillets	4-5	Salmon (Whole, 1kg/2.2lbs)	10-15
Halibut and Turbot Steaks and Fillets	4-5	Salmon Steaks and Tail pieces	2-7
Smoked Fish (poached)	1-2	Sea Bass (Whole, 1kg/2.2lbs)	10-15
Sole Fillets	2-3	Prawns/Shrimp Scampi/Langoustines	2-5
Mackerel	10-12	Scallops	2-5
Trout	8-10	Mussels	2-3
Herring Fillets	6-8	Oysters	1-2
Tuna Steaks	5	Squid	6
Monkfish Tail Portion	8-9		
Sliced	2-5		

Whole fish can be "fried" in a browning dish. They can also be cooked in bags, shallow covered dishes or enclosed in greaseproof paper — en papillote.

Shellfish can toughen if cooked too quickly at too high a temperature. Add them to a hot sauce and leave for 5 minutes to cook in residual heat. Alternatively, cook on their own for no more than 3 minutes.

See chart No. 4 for times and settings.

Cooking Vegetables

Microwave cooking is ideal for vegetables. Very little water is needed, so they keep their colour and nutrients. They are best cooked loosely covered, and whole vegetables like corn-on-the-cob, aubergines, artichokes and chicory can be completely wrapped in cling film and cooked without any water. Cooking bags are another alternative.

Break broccoli into even-sized pieces and, if cooking a large quantity, be sure to put the flower ends in toward the centre of the dish. Trim down the tough ends of asparagus and peel the ends of the stalks. This will help the stalks cook quickly before the tips are overcooked. Some vegetables, like cucumbers, spring onions and button onions cook very well in butter or margarine alone, if well covered. Chart No. 5 lists suggested cooking times.

Cooking Fruit

Poach, bake and preserve fruit with ease in a microwave oven. Sterilise jars for preserving by adding a little water and heating on High for about 2-3 minutes and then draining. Metal lids and rubbers seals are best sterilised outside the microwave oven.

CHART 5 Cooking Vegetables

Type	Quantity	Water	Mins. on High	Mins. Stdg. Time
Artichokes	4	430ml/¾pt/1½ cups	10-20	5
Asparagus	450g/1lb	140ml/¼pt/½ cup	9-12	5
Aubergine/ Eggplant	2 med.	30ml/2 tbsps	7-10	5
Beans Green, French	450g/1lb	140ml/¼pt/½ cup	8	3
Broad/Lima			10	3
Beetroot/Beets Whole	2	60ml/2 fl oz/¼ cup	4-5	3
Broccoli	450g/1lb	140ml/¼ pt/½ cup	4-5	3
Brussels Sprouts	450g/1lb	60ml/2 fl oz/¼ cup	8-10	3-5
Cabbage Shredded	450g/1lb	140ml/¼ pint/½ cup	7-9	3
Quartered			9-12	5
Carrots Whole	225g/8oz	140ml/¼ pint/½ cup	10	6
Sliced			7	5
Cauliflower	450g/1lb			
Whole		280ml/½ pint/1 cup	11	3
Florets		140ml/¼ pint/½ cup	7	3
Chicory	4	60ml/2 fl oz/¼ cup (water or stock)	5	3
Corn-on-the-Cob	2 ears	60ml/2 fl oz/¼ cup	6	3
Courgettes/ Zucchini	450g/1lb	60ml/2 fl oz/¼ cup	5	3
Fennel Sliced	1 bulb	280ml/½ pint/1 cup boiling water	2-8	3
Quartered			10-12	3
Leeks, sliced	450g/1lb	140ml/¼ pint/½ cup	7-10	3
Mushrooms	225g/8oz	30ml/2 tbsps	2	3
Okra	225g/8oz	60ml/2 fl oz/¼ cup	4	3
Onions, small	225g/8oz	30ml/1 fl oz/2 tbsps	7-8	3
Sliced	2	60ml/2 fl oz/¼ cup	10	3
Parsnips	225g/8oz	140ml/¼ pint/½ cup	8-10	3
Peas, shelled	450g/1lb	140ml/¼ pint/½ cup	10-15	5
Peapods/ Mangetout	225g/8oz	140ml/¼ pint/½ cup	3	3
Peppers	2 sliced	60ml/2 fl oz/¼ cup	3	3
Potatoes New	450g/1lb	140ml/¼ pint/½ cup	10-12	5
Baked	2		9-12	10
Boiled	450g/1lb	140ml/¼ pint/½ cup	6-7	5
Spinach	225g/8oz		4-5	3
Turnips	225g/8oz	60ml/2 fl oz/¼ cup	12	3

Paraffin wax for sealing jars cannot be melted in a microwave oven. The great advantages of microwave preserving are that jams and jellies can be made in small amounts and the job is much less messy and time-consuming. Whole preserved fruits and pickled vegetables can't be heated long enough to kill bacteria, so they must be kept refrigerated after bottling.

Cooking Rice, Pasta, Grains and Pulses

Rice and pasta need nearly as much cooking by microwave methods as by conventional ones. However, both pasta and rice cook without sticking together and without the chance of overcooking. This is because most of the actual cooking is accomplished during standing time. All kinds of rice and shapes of pasta benefit from being put into hot water with a pinch of salt and 5ml/1 tsp oil in a deep bowl. There is no need to cover the bowl during cooking, but, during standing time, a covering of some sort will help retain heat. Ease long spaghetti into the bowl gradually as it softens. Drain rice and pasta and rinse under hot water to remove starch. Both pasta and rice can be reheated in a microwave oven without loss of texture. Fresh pasta doesn't seem to take to the microwave oven successfully.

There is a great time saving with dried peas, beans and lentils — pulses. Cover them with water in a large bowl and heat on a High setting to bring to the boil, which takes about 10 minutes. Allow the pulses to boil for about 2 minutes and then leave to stand for one hour. This cuts out overnight soaking. The pulses will cook in about 45 minutes to one hour depending on what variety is used. This is about half the conventional cooking time. Make sure pulses are cooked completely; it can be dangerous to eat them undercooked. Refer to Chart No. 6 for cooking times.

Cooking Eggs and Cheese

When poaching eggs, always pierce the yolks with a skewer or fork to prevent them from bursting. Use individual ramekins or patty pans with a spoonful of water in each. Alternatively, bring water to the boil in a large dish and add a pinch of salt and 5ml/1 tsp vinegar to help set the egg whites. Slip the eggs in one at a time. Cook just until the whites are set. To stop the cooking and to keep the eggs from drying out, keep them in a bowl of cold water. For frying eggs, choose a browning dish, and for

Microwave ovens can cut the rising time for yeast doughs nearly in half, and a loaf of bread will bake in an astonishing 8-10 minutes.

Biscuits will not usually crisp in a microwave oven except in one with a combination setting. However, they bake to a moist, chewy texture which is just as pleasing. A batch of 3 dozen will cook in about 10 minutes.

Pastry is not as much of a problem as most people believe. Prick the base and sides of the pastry well, after lining a pie or flan dish. It is essential to bake the pastry shell "blind" — without filling — in order to dry the base. Pastry will not bake to an even brown. The exception is, of course, pastry baked in a combination oven. Pastry and filling can be baked at the same time in these ovens.

CHART 6 Cooking Rice, Pasta, Grains and Pulses

Type	Quantity	Water	Mins. on High	Mins. Stdg. Time
Brown Rice	120g/4oz/ 1 cup	570ml/1 pint/ 2 cups	20	5
White Rice (long grain)	120g/4oz/ 1 cup	570ml/1 pint/ 2 cups	10-12	5
Quick Cooking Rice	120g/4oz/ 1 cup	430ml/¾ pint/ 1½ cups	6	5
Macaroni	225g/8oz/ 3 cups	1 litre/1¾ pints/ 3½ cups	6	10
Quick Cooking Macaroni	225g/8oz/ 3 cups	1 litre/1¾ pints/ 3½ cups	3	10
Spaghetti	225g/8oz	1 litre/1¾ pints/ 3½ cups	6-10	10
Tagliatelle/Fettucine	225g/8oz	1 litre/1¾ pints/ 3½ cups	5-9	10
Pasta Shapes	225g/8oz/ 3 cups	1 litre/1¾ pints/ 3½ cups	6	10
Lasagne Ravioli Cannelloni	180g-225g/ 6oz-8oz	1 litre/1¾ pints/ 3½ cups	6	10
Barley	120g/4oz/ 1 cup	570ml/1 pint/ 2 cups	20	10
Bulgur (cracked wheat)	225g/8oz/ 2 cups	570ml/1 pint/ 2 cups boiling water	4	10
Dried Beans	180g/6oz/ 1 cup	1 litre/1¾ pints/ 3½ cups	55-60	10
Dried Peas	225g/8oz/ 3 cups	1 litre/1¾ pints/ 3½ cups	45-60	10
Lentils	225g/8oz/ 3 cups	1 litre/1¾ pints/ 3½ cups	20-25	15

NOTE: Add a pinch of salt and 5ml/1 tsp oil to grains and pasta

scrambling use a deep bowl or glass measuring jug. Always remove scrambled eggs from the oven while they are still very soft. Stir during standing time to finish cooking. Hollandaise sause is easy to make. Choose the same kind of container as for scrambled eggs and have a bowl of iced water ready. Use a medium setting and cook the sauce at short intervals, whisking vigorously in between times. Put the sauce bowl into the iced water at the first sign of curdling or briefly when it has thickened, to stop the cooking process.

Cheese will get very stringy if it overcooks or gets too hot. When preparing a cheese sauce, stir finely grated cheese into the hot sauce base and leave to stand. The cheese will melt without further cooking. Cheese toppings will not brown except in a combination oven. A medium setting is best for cheese.

Baking

Baking is one of the most surprising things a microwave oven does. Quick breads, those leavened with baking powder or soda and sour milk, rise higher than they do in a conventional oven and bake faster. If using a square or loaf dish, cover the corners with foil for part of the cooking time to keep that part of the bread or cake from drying out before the middle is cooked. Cakes also rise much higher and a single layer will bake in about 6 minutes on a medium setting.

CHART 7 Reheating

	Quantity	Setting	Time from room temp. (minutes)	Special Instructions		Quantity	Setting	Time from room temp. (minutes)	Special Instructions
Spaghetti Sauce	225g/8oz 450g/1lb	Med.	5-6 7-8	Stir several times. Keep loosely covered.	Pasta	120g/4oz 225g/8oz	Med. or High	2-3 5-6	Stir once or twice. Add 5ml/ 1 tsp oil. Use shorter time for High setting.
Beef Stew	225g/8oz 450g/1lb	Med.	5-5½ 6-7	Stir occasionally. Cover loosely.	Rice	120g/4oz 225g/8oz	Med. or High	2-3 4-5	Stir once or twice. Add 5ml/ 1 tsp oil or butter. Use shorter time for High setting.
Casseroles	225g/8oz 450g/1lb	Med.	5-7 7-8	Stir occasionally. Cover loosely. Use the shorter time for chicken, fish or vegetables.	Potatoes	120g/4oz 225g/8oz 450g/1lb	High	1-2 2-3 3-4	Use the shorter time for mashed potatoes. Do not reheat fried potatoes. Cover loosely.
Chili	225g/8oz 450g/1lb	Med.	5-5½ 6-7	Stir several times. Keep loosely covered.	Corn-on-the-Cob	2 ears 4 ears	High	2-3 4-6	Wrap in plastic wrap/cling film
Pork Chops	2 4	Med.	5 7½	Turn over halfway through. Cover loosely.	Carrots	225g/8oz 450g/1lb	High	1-2 2-4	Cover loosely. Stir once.
Lamb Chops	2 4	Med.	4-5 6-10	Turn over halfway through. Cover loosely.	Turnips	225g/8oz 450g/1lb	High	1-2 2-4	Cover loosely. Stir carefully.
Sliced beef, pork, veal	120g/4oz 225g/8oz	Med.	3-5 6-7½	Add gravy or sauce if possible. Cover loosely.	Broccoli Asparagus	120g/4oz 225g/8oz	High	2 2	Cover loosely. Rearrange once.
Sliced turkey, chicken, ham	120g/4oz 225g/8oz	Med.	2½-5 4-6	Add gravy or sauce if possible. Cover loosely.	Peas Beans Courgettes/ Zucchini	120g/4oz 225g/8oz	High	1-1½ 1½-2	Cover loosely. Stir occasionally.

To let air and heat circulate underneath breads, cakes and pastry shells, place them on a rack or inverted saucer. This allows the base to cook faster and more evenly. Once baked and cool, keep microwave-baked goods well covered. They seem to dry out faster than those conventionally baked.

Defrosting and Reheating

With the defrosting and reheating abilities of a microwave oven menu planning can become crisis-free. Most ovens incorporate an automatic defrosting control into their setting programs. If your oven does not have this facility, use the lowest temperature setting and employ an on/off technique. In other words, turn the oven on at 30 second-1 minute intervals and let the food stand for a minute or two before repeating the process. This procedure allows the food to defrost evenly without starting to cook at the edges. The times given in Charts No. 7 and 8 apply to ovens of 600-700 watts.

Always cover the food when defrosting or reheating. Plastic containers, plastic bags and freezer-to-table ware can be used to freeze and defrost food in. Meals can be placed on paper or plastic trays and frozen. Cover with cling film or greaseproof paper. Usually, foods are better defrosted first and cooked or reheated second. There are exceptions to this rule, so be sure to check instructions on pre-packaged foods before proceeding. Food frozen in blocks, such as spinach or casseroles, should be broken up as they defrost.

Breads, rolls and coffee cakes can be placed on paper plates or covered in paper towels to reheat or defrost. These materials will help protect the foods and absorb moisture which will come to the surface and could make these foods soggy. If you want a crisp crust on reheated bread, slip a sheet of foil under the paper towel and don't cover completely.

When reheating foods in a sauce, stir occasionally to distribute heat evenly. Spread food out in an even layer for uniform heating. Sauces and gravies can be poured over sliced meat and poultry to keep it moist while reheating. Vegetables, except for root vegetables and starchy ones like corn, lose texture when they are reheated. It is best to add them at the last

CHART 8 Defrosting

	Mins. on Low/ Defrost Setting per 450g/1lb	Mins. Stdg. Time	Instructions
Pork, Veal, Lamb, Beef for Roasting	8-10	30-40	Pierce covering. Turn frequently.
Ground/ Minced Beef or Lamb	7-8	5-6	Pierce wrapping. Break up as it defrosts.
Hamburgers	6-8	5	Use shorter time if individually wrapped. Pierce wrapper and separate when starting to defrost. Turn patties over once.
Bacon	6-8	5	Cover in paper towels. Separate as slices defrost.
Sausages	6-8	5	Cover in paper towels. Separate as defrosting.
Whole Chickens, Duck, Game Birds	5-7	30	Pierce wrapper. Remove giblets as soon as possible. Cover leg ends, wings, breast bone with foil part of the time. Turn several times.
Poultry Pieces	6-8	15-20	Pierce wrapper. Turn several times.
Casseroles, filled crêpes (for 4 people)	4-10	10	Defrost in dish, loosely covered. Stir casseroles if possible.

	Mins. on Low/ Defrost Setting per 450g/1lb	Mins. Stdg. Time	Instructions
Vegetables	1-8	3-5	Cover loosely. Break up or stir occasionally.
Fish Fillets and Steaks	6-10	5-10	Pierce wrapper. Separate during defrosting. Use greater time for steaks.
Whole Fish	6-8	10	Pierce wrapper. Turn over during defrosting. Cover tail with foil halfway through.
Shellfish	6-8	6	Pierce wrapper. Stir or break up pieces during defrosting.
Bread Loaf	2-4 (per average loaf)	5-10	Cover with paper towels. Turn over once.
1 Slice Bread	20 seconds	1	Cover in paper towels.
Rolls 6	1½-3	3	Cover in paper towels. Turn over once.
12	2-4	5	
Cake	1½-2	2	Place on serving plate. Some icings not suitable.
Fruit Pie 23cm/9″	8-10	6	Use a glass dish. Place on inverted saucer or rack.

minute to other foods. To tell if reheating is completed, touch the bottom of the plate or container. If it feels hot, then the food is ready.

Foods can be arranged on plates in advance and reheated very successfully, an advantage when entertaining. With a microwave oven, you can spend more time with your guests than by yourself in the kitchen!

Recipe Conversion

Experiment with your favourite recipes and you will probably find that many of them can be converted for microwave cooking with only a few changes. Things that don't work are recipes which call for whipped egg whites, such as angel food cake and crisp meringue shells. Soft meringues for pies will work, and one of the most amazing recipe conversions is that for crisp meringues. These meringues triple in size as they cook and are made from a fondant-like mixture.

Batters for pancakes, waffles or Yorkshire pudding are impossible to cook successfully. Deep fat frying is understandably impossible. Yeast doughs and biscuit doughs must be specially formulated for microwave cooking. To convert your own recipes, the following rules will help:

* Look for similar microwave recipes with the same quantities of solid ingredients, dish size, techniques and times.

* Reduce liquid quantities by one quarter. More can always be added later in cooking.

* Cut down on fat and save calories as well as cooking time. Fat will attract microwave energy and slow down the cooking of the other ingredients in the recipe.

* Reduce the seasoning in your recipe; microwave cooking intensifies flavours.

* Microwave cooking takes approximately a quarter of the time of conventional cooking. Allow at least 5 minutes standing time before checking to see if the food is cooked. You can always add more time at this point if necessary.

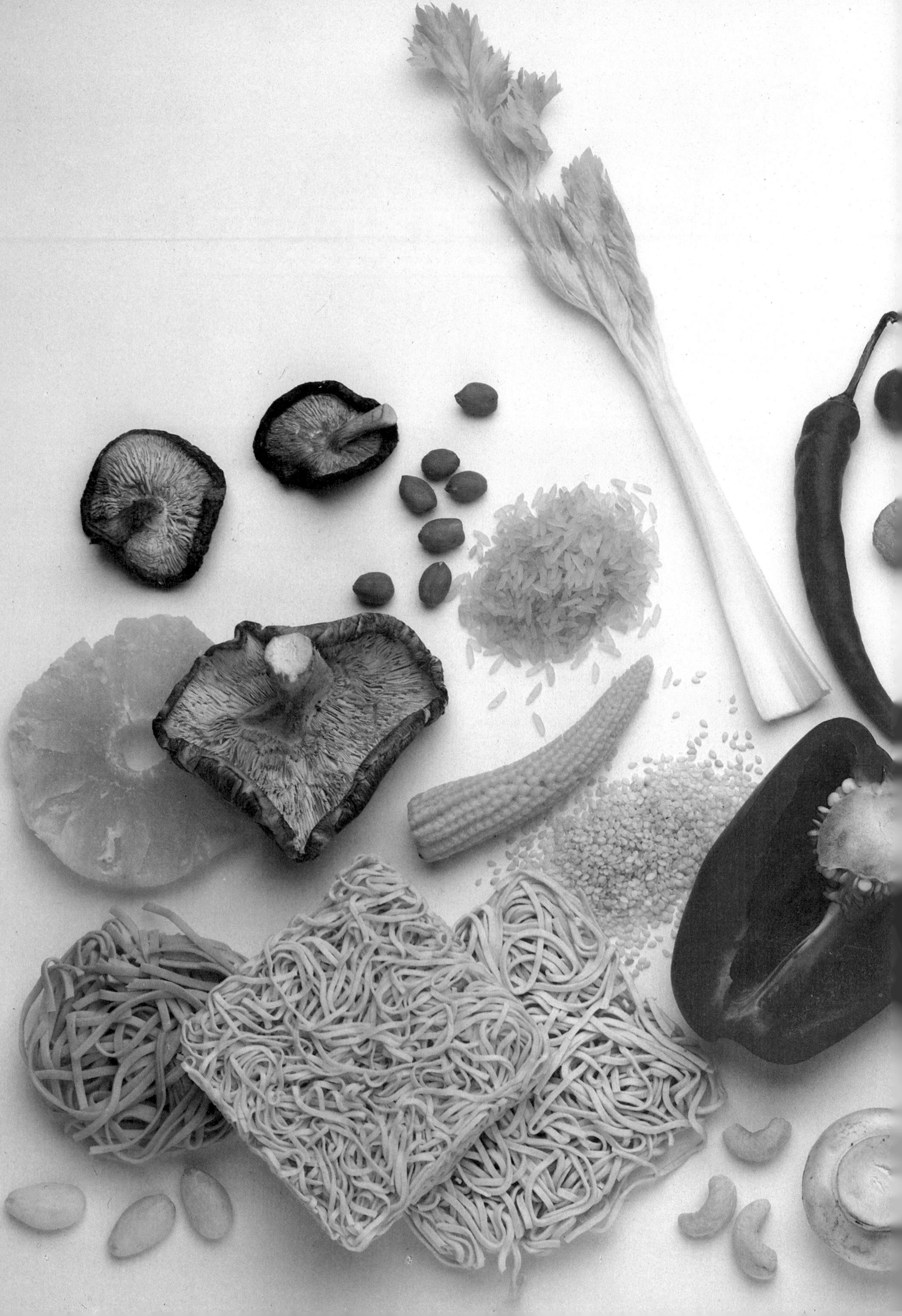

Microwave
CHINESE COOKING

Chinese cooking means fast cooking. Microwave cooking does, too, so why not combine them. Many classic Chinese specialities are possible with a microwave oven. The usual cornflour/cornstarch based Chinese sauces need more thickening because liquids evaporate less in microwave cooking, but otherwise they are easy to do. Stir-frying transfers successfully from the wok to the browning dish, and you can even achieve a stir-fried effect without one.

Garnishes for Chinese dishes tend to be very simple. These two are easy to do and can be prepared in advance:

Chili flowers: Choose small red or green chili peppers. Cut in thin strips, lengthwise, to within 1.25-2.5cm/½-1 inch of the stem. Keep the stem end intact and carefully remove seeds and core. Place in ice water for several hours or overnight until the "petals" open up. Eat at your own risk!

Spring/green onion brushes: Trim the onions into 7.5-10cm/3-4 inch lengths. Cut the greener end into thin strips and leave white "bulb" end intact. Alternatively, cut both ends into the thin strips, leaving 1.25cm/½ inch of the middle intact. Soak as for chili flowers.

For a taste of China from your microwave oven, look for these ingredients:

Bamboo shoots – First growth of the bamboo plant, cut just as it emerges from the ground. Crisp, ivory-coloured and slightly sweet, usually sold canned, sliced or in whole pieces which can be cut to various shapes.

Baby sweetcorn – Miniature variety of corn. Sold in cans and often available fresh. Needs very brief cooking.

Black beans – Used often in Cantonese cooking. Available in pre-prepared sauce or salted to preserve them. Salted beans should be soaked.

Chili peppers – Available dried or fresh. Usually red, they are often used in Szechuan cooking. Seeds are the hottest part, so remove for less heat.

Chili sauce – Available hot or sweet and made from fresh, red chili peppers.

Chinese leaves/cabbage – Called leaves in England and cabbage in America, usually refers to Chinese celery cabbage. Some varieties have thicker, whiter spines. Readily available in greengrocers or supermarkets. Smaller, stronger-tasting bok choy is rarely seen outside Chinese markets.

Chinese parsley – Also coriander leaves or cilantro. A pungent green herb with a leaf similar to flat parsley.

Five-spice powder – A combination of star anise, anise pepper, fennel, cloves and cinnamon. Use sparingly.

Ginger – Knobbly root that must be peeled before use. Use grated or thinly sliced in small amounts. Powdered variety available, and preserved pieces in sugar syrup.

Hoisin sauce – Used often in Chinese barbecue cooking. A thick vegetable-based sauce. Useful for stir-fried dishes and a dipping sauce as well.

Lotus – Root is available canned or fresh from Chinese groceries. Cut in thin rounds, it has a flower-like shape. Obtained from waterlilies. Seeds are available preserved or fresh at the Chinese New Year and reputedly bring good luck. Leaves are available from Chinese groceries to cook in or on. Should be soaked first.

Mushrooms, dried Chinese – Brown-black in colour, must be soaked 15-30 minutes before use. Stronger in taste than fresh mushrooms, they also have a chewier texture.

Red bean paste – Made from boiled red beans or bean flour mixed with water and lard. Usually sweetened and used in desserts.

Red wine – Available from Chinese groceries, it has a flavour ranging from dry sherry to sweet white wine, depending on the variety brought. Substitute either sherry or white wine.

Rice vinegar – Made from rice and quite pale in colour. Substitute white wine vinegar.

Sesame oil – Pressed from sesame seeds, it is golden in colour with a nutty flavour. Expensive, so use as a flavouring at the end of cooking.

Sesame paste – Also called tahini and used in Middle-Eastern cooking as well. Thick, whitish paste, about the consistency of peanut butter and tasing of sesame seeds.

Soy sauce – Made from fermented soy beans. There are various strengths which will effect the colour and flavour of the finished dish.

Star anise – Star shaped seed pod with a liquorice taste. Used in meat, poultry and sweet dishes.

Szechuan peppercorns – Also called wild pepper. Not readily available, so substitute black peppercorns.

Water chestnuts – Fresh variety is very difficult to obtain. Usually found canned, peeled, sliced or whole. Creamy white in colour and crisp in texture.

White radish or Mooli – Very large. Delicious crisp texture and white translucent appearance. Barely needs cooking.

Wonton skins or wrappers – Thin sheets of egg noodle dough in large or small squares. The traditional wrapping for spring rolls and dumplings with various stuffings. Can be steamed or cooked in liquid.

Wood or tree ears – Greyish black tree fungus. Sold dried and must be soaked before use.

Yellow beans – Whole in brine, paste or sauce form. They are golden brown in colour and very salty.

NOTE: Recipes were tested in a 650 watt maximum oven. HIGH = Full or 100%, MEDIUM = 50%, LOW/DEFROST = 25%.

Microwave
CHINESE COOKING

SAUCES, RICE AND NOODLES

Hot Mustard Sauce

PREPARATION TIME: 10 minutes

MICROWAVE COOKING TIME:
4 minutes

MAKES: About 200ml/6 fl oz/
3-4 cups

60g/4 tbsps dry mustard
60ml/4 tbsps rice wine vinegar
7.5ml/1½ tsps cornflour/cornstarch
120ml/4 fl oz/½ cup water
45ml/3 tbsps honey
Salt

Mix the mustard and cornflour/
cornstarch together. Beat in the water,
vinegar and honey gradually until
smooth. Add a small pinch of salt
and cook, uncovered, in a small, deep
bowl for 4 minutes on HIGH. Stir
every 30 seconds until thickened.
Serve with starters/appetizers or
seafood.

Pineapple Sauce

PREPARATION TIME: 10-15 minutes

MICROWAVE COOKING TIME:
4 minutes

MAKES: About 570ml/1 pint/2 cups

225g/8oz can crushed pineapple, or
*   1 fresh pineapple, peeled and cored*
7.5ml/1½ tsp cornflour/cornstarch
*   dissolved in 15ml/1 tbsp water*
15ml/1 tbsp light soy sauce
7.5ml/1½ tsp sugar
15ml/1 tbsp white wine
1 piece ginger root, grated
Pinch salt

If using fresh pineapple, work in a

food processor until finely chopped.
Add remaining ingredients and mix
well in a small, deep bowl. Cook
4 minutes on HIGH until the sauce
thickens and clears. Serve with duck
or prawns/shrimp.

**This page: Pineapple Sauce (top)
and Plum Sauce (bottom). Facing
page: Hot Mustard Sauce (top)
and Sweet and Sour Sauce
(bottom).**

Plum Sauce

PREPARATION TIME: 10-15 minutes

MICROWAVE COOKING TIME:
10 minutes

MAKES: About 570ml/1 pint/2 cups

225g/8oz canned plums, stoned, or fresh
plums, halved and stoned
225g/8oz/1 cup apricot jam
60ml/2 fl oz/¼ cup rice wine vinegar
10ml/2 tsp cornflour/cornstarch
2.5ml/½ tsp five-spice powder

Combine all the ingredients in a large
bowl or casserole. If using canned
plums, include the juice, and cook
5 minutes on HIGH until the sauce
thickens and clears. Purée until
smooth in a food processor, if
desired. If using fresh plums, add
60ml/2 fl oz/¼ cup water to the
ingredients and reserve the
cornflour/cornstarch until later.
Cook the plums, covered, for
5 minutes on HIGH until soft. Mix
the cornflour/cornstarch and vinegar,
add to the plums and proceed as for
canned plums. Serve with pork or
duck.

Shanghai Noodle Snack

PREPARATION TIME: 15 minutes

MICROWAVE COOKING TIME:
5-6 minutes plus 5 minutes
standing time

SERVES: 6 people

450g/1lb Chinese egg noodles
1150ml/2 pints/4 cups boiling water

SAUCE
30ml/2 tbsps cornflour/cornstarch
dissolved in 60ml/2 fl oz/¼ cup water
30ml/2 tbsps rice wine
15ml/1 tbsp light soy sauce
280ml/½ pint/1 cup light stock
1 small piece ginger root, thinly sliced
4 spring/green onions, thinly sliced
diagonally
Meat from one large crab or 1 180g/6oz
package frozen or canned crabmeat

Cook the noodles in the boiling
water for 3 minutes on HIGH. Leave
to stand 5 minutes, covered, while
preparing the sauce. Combine the
first 5 ingredients in a deep bowl,
stirring well to mix the cornflour/
cornstarch. Cook 2-3 minutes until
the sauce thickens and clears. Add
the crab and onion and cook
30 seconds on HIGH. Drain the
noodles well and toss with the sauce
to serve.

Velvet Noodles

PREPARATION TIME: 20 minutes

MICROWAVE COOKING TIME:
8-12 minutes plus 5 minutes
standing time

SERVES: 6 people

25ml/1½ tbsps light soy sauce
15ml/1 tbsp cornflour/cornstarch
Dash sesame oil
90g/3oz lean pork cut in small, thin slices
60g/2oz/½ cup mushrooms, sliced
570ml/1 pint/2 cups chicken stock
Salt
1150ml/2 pints/4 cups boiling water
450g/1lb/2 packages medium Chinese
noodles
½ head Chinese leaves/cabbage, shredded

Mix soy sauce, cornflour/cornstarch
and sesame oil together in a large
bowl. Stir in the stock gradually and
add the pork and mushrooms. Cover
and cook for 5-8 minutes on HIGH
or until pork is cooked. Add the
Chinese leaves/cabbage and leave to
stand, covered, while cooking the
noodles. Put the noodles and water
into a large, deep bowl. Cook for
3 minutes on HIGH, stirring
occasionally. Leave to stand
5 minutes before serving. Add salt to
the mushrooms and pork if desired.
Drain the noodles and arrange on a
serving dish. Pour over the sauce and
toss before serving.

Tossed Noodles

PREPARATION TIME: 20 minutes

MICROWAVE COOKING TIME:
10 minutes plus 5 minutes
standing time

SERVES: 6 people

450g/1lb Chinese egg noodles
1150ml/2 pints/4 cups boiling water

120ml/4oz/½ cup soy sauce mixed with
30ml/2 tbsps cornflour/cornstarch
90g/3oz lean steak, cut in short, thin
strips
15ml/1 tbsp oil
120ml/4 fl oz/½ cup brown stock
4 spring/green onions, sliced
½ cucumber, sliced
1 small piece white radish, diced
Fresh coriander leaves (Chinese parsley)

Cook noodles as for Velvet Noodles.
Heat a browning dish 5 minutes on
HIGH. Pour in the oil and add the
steak. Cook 2 minutes on HIGH. Stir
in the soy sauce, cornflour/
cornstarch and the stock. Cover and
cook 3 minutes on HIGH. Add more
stock if the sauce is too thick. Add
the onions, cucumber and radish to
the sauce, and leave to stand
5 minutes before serving. Pour over
noodles and toss before serving.
Garnish with whole coriander leaves.

Ham and Bean Fried Rice

PREPARATION TIME: 15 minutes

MICROWAVE COOKING TIME:
9 minutes plus 2 minutes
standing time

SERVES: 4 people

45ml/3 tbsps oil
2 eggs, beaten
Salt and pepper
120g/4oz/½ cup ham, chopped
120g/4oz French/green beans, cut in
thin, diagonal slices
225g/8oz/3 cups cooked rice
15ml/1 tbsp soy sauce
4 spring/green onions, chopped

Heat a browning dish 5 minutes on
HIGH. Pour in half the oil and half
the beaten egg and cook for

**Facing page: Shanghai Noodle
Snack.**

30 seconds on HIGH on one side.
Turn over and cook for 30 seconds
on the second side. Repeat with
remaining egg. Keep the egg warm
and add the remaining oil to the dish.
Heat for 1 minute on HIGH and add
the ham. Cover the dish and cook
for 1 minute on HIGH. Add the rice
and cook, covered, for 5 minutes on
HIGH. Add the beans, soy sauce and
onions. Cook 1 minute on HIGH and
toss the ingredients to mix well. Slice
the eggs into thin strips and scatter
over the top of the rice. Cover the
dish and leave to stand for 2 minutes
before serving.

Subgum Fried Rice

PREPARATION TIME: 15 minutes

MICROWAVE COOKING TIME:
7 minutes plus 2 minutes
standing time

SERVES: 4 people

45ml/3 tbsps oil
225g/8oz/3 cups cooked rice
2 sticks celery, cut into small dice
60g/2oz/½ cup mushrooms, roughly
    chopped
½ red pepper, diced
3 eggs, beaten
15ml/1 tbsp light soy sauce
Dash sesame oil
Salt and pepper

GARNISH
2 spring/green onions, sliced diagonally

Heat oil in a large bowl for 1 minute
on HIGH. Add the rice and cook
5 minutes on HIGH, covered. Stir in
the eggs, soy sauce and vegetables
and cook 2 minutes on HIGH. Add
the sesame oil, salt and pepper and
leave to stand 2 minutes before
serving. Garnish with onions.

Eight Precious Rice

PREPARATION TIME: 20 minutes

MICROWAVE COOKING TIME:
10 minutes plus 2 minutes
standing time

SERVES: 4 people

45ml/3 tbsps oil
120g/4oz chicken, cut in 1.25cm/½ inch
    cubes
120g/4oz frozen peas
60g/2oz prawns/shrimp
30g/1oz/¼ cup diced bamboo shoots
8 water chestnuts, sliced thinly
60g/2oz/½ cup mushrooms, sliced thinly
4 spring/green onions, chopped
225g/8oz/3 cups cooked rice
2 eggs, beaten
30ml/2 tbsps soy sauce
Salt and pepper

Heat oil in a large bowl 1 minute on

HIGH. Add the chicken and cook,
stirring frequently, for 3 minutes on
HIGH. Cover the bowl loosely. Add
the rice and cook 5 minutes on
HIGH to heat through. Add the
remaining ingredients and cook
1 minute on HIGH. Leave to stand,
covered, 2 minutes before serving.

**This page: Eight Precious Rice
(top) and Ham and Bean Fried
Rice (bottom). Facing page: Tossed
Noodles (top) and Velvet Noodles
(bottom).**

Sweet and Sour Sauce

PREPARATION TIME: 10 minutes
MICROWAVE COOKING TIME: 4 minutes
MAKES: 280ml/½ pint/1 cup

280ml/½ pint/1 cup pineapple or orange
  juice
15g/1 tbsp brown sugar
15g/1 tbsp cornflour/cornstarch
1 clove garlic, minced
15ml/1 tbsp vinegar
15ml/1 tbsp soy sauce
10ml/2 tsps ketchup
Salt and pepper

Combine all the ingredients in a deep
bowl or glass measure. Cook 4
minutes on HIGH, stirring often after
1 minute, until the sauce thickens and
clears. Serve with starters/appetizers,
seafood, pork or chicken.

Fried Rice with Egg

PREPARATION TIME: 15 minutes
MICROWAVE COOKING TIME: 8-10 minutes plus standing time
SERVES: 4 people

45ml/3 tbsps oil
2 spring/green onions, finely chopped
225g/8oz/3 cups cooked rice
3 eggs, beaten
10ml/2 tsps white wine
Salt and pepper
Dash sesame oil
GARNISH
2 spring/green onions, shredded

Put the oil and the finely chopped
onions into a large bowl and heat for
1 minute on HIGH. Add the rice and
cook for 5-7 minutes on HIGH, until
very hot. Stir in the eggs, wine, salt,
pepper and sesame oil and cook for
2 minutes on HIGH. Stir carefully
and leave to stand, covered, several
minutes before serving. Garnish with
the shredded onions. Serve with soy
sauce, or as an accompaniment to
other dishes.

**Fried Rice with Egg (top) and
Subgum Rice (bottom).**

SOUPS AND APPETIZERS

Sweetcorn and Crabmeat Soup

PREPARATION TIME: 10 minutes

MICROWAVE COOKING TIME:
4 minutes plus 5 minutes
standing time

SERVES: 4 people

2 225g/8oz cans creamed corn
1 onion
1150ml/2 pints/4 cups chicken stock
1 small piece ginger root, peeled and
   grated
5ml/1 tsp sherry
30ml/2 tbsps cornflour/cornstarch
225g/8oz crabmeat
2 spring/green onions
Salt

Combine the onion and corn in a
deep bowl. Cover and cook 1 minute
on HIGH to soften onion slightly.
Add the ginger, sherry, stock and
cornflour/cornstarch mixed with
30ml/2 tbsps water. Cook for 2-3
minutes until thickened, stirring
halfway through cooking. Stir in the
crabmeat, reserving about 30ml/
2 tbsps for garnish. Leave to stand,
covered, for 3 minutes before
serving. Sprinkle reserved crabmeat
and spring/green onion on top of
each serving.

**This page: Chinese Noodle Soup
with Pork Dumplings (top) and
Sweetcorn and Crabmeat Soup
(bottom). Facing page: Chicken
Corn Chowder with Almonds
(top) and Soup of Mushrooms and
Peas (bottom).**

Wonton Soup

PREPARATION TIME: 20 minutes

MICROWAVE COOKING TIME:
17-18 minutes

SERVES: 4 people

12 wonton skins
90g/3oz minced/ground pork
2 spring/green onions, finely chopped
5ml/1 tsp garlic, finely chopped
Pinch five-spice powder
1 egg, beaten
1150ml/2 pints/4 cups chicken stock
30ml/2 tbsps light soy sauce
½ head Chinese leaves/cabbage

Heat the chicken stock 10 minutes on HIGH. Mix pork, onions, garlic, spice powder and stuff the wonton skins. Brush the edges with beaten egg. Fold wontons in triangles and seal well. Combine the water and soy sauce in a large, deep bowl and add the stuffed wontons. Partially cover the bowl and cook 5-6 minutes on HIGH, or until wontons are tender. Add the shredded Chinese leaves/cabbage and cook a further 2-3 minutes on HIGH.

Chinese Noodle Soup with Pork Dumplings

PREPARATION TIME: 20 minutes

MICROWAVE COOKING TIME:
10 minutes plus 1 minute standing time

SERVES: 4 people

225g/8oz minced/ground pork
2.5ml/½ tsp ground ginger
15ml/1 tbsp cornflour/cornstarch
30ml/2 tbsps light soy sauce
1150ml/2 pints/4 cups stock
60g/2oz or ¼ package thin Chinese noodles
15ml/1 tbsp rice wine
4 spring/green onions, sliced

Mix the cornflour/cornstarch with the soy sauce. Combine with the pork and ginger. Shape into small balls. Heat the stock 5 minutes on HIGH in a large, deep bowl. Add the pork balls and cook 2 minutes on HIGH. Add the noodles and wine and cook a further 3 minutes on HIGH. Add the spring/green onions and leave to stand 1 minute before serving.

Chicken Corn Chowder with Almonds

PREPARATION TIME: 15 minutes

MICROWAVE COOKING TIME:
5-8 minutes

SERVES: 4 people

2 225g/8oz cans creamed corn
1150ml/2 pints/4 cups chicken stock
2 chicken breasts, finely chopped
30ml/2 tbsps cornflour/cornstarch
30ml/2 tbsps rice wine
60g/2oz/½ cup toasted almonds
Salt and pepper

Combine corn, stock and chicken in a large, deep bowl. Partially cover and cook 3-5 minutes or until chicken is nearly cooked. Combine rice wine, cornflour/cornstarch and stir into the soup. Cook 2-3 minutes to allow cornflour/cornstarch to thicken and clear. Sprinkle with toasted almonds and serve.

Prawn/Shrimp and Lettuce Soup

PREPARATION TIME: 10 minutes

MICROWAVE COOKING TIME:
12 minutes plus 5 minutes standing time

SERVES: 4 people

360g/12oz peeled prawns/shrimp
120g/4oz/1 cup rice
1150ml/2 pints/4 cups hot chicken stock
1 piece fresh ginger root, grated
1 small head lettuce, shredded
Salt

Put the rice, stock and ginger into a large, deep bowl. Partially cover and cook 12 minutes on HIGH, stirring often. Cook until the rice softens completely. Add the prawns/shrimp, lettuce and salt. Leave the soup to stand, covered, for 5 minutes. Prawns/shrimp should heat through in the stock.

Soup of Mushrooms and Peas

PREPARATION TIME: 15 minutes

MICROWAVE COOKING TIME:
10 minutes

SERVES: 4 people

12 dried Chinese mushrooms, soaked 30 minutes
120g/4oz ham, shredded
1150ml/2 pints/4 cups light stock
15ml/1 tbsp light soy sauce
225g/8oz/2 cups fresh peas
Salt and pepper

Remove the stems and slice the mushrooms finely. Combine with the remaining ingredients and cook 10 minutes on HIGH or until peas are just tender.

Facing page: Prawn/Shrimp and Lettuce Soup (top) and Wonton Soup (bottom).

Steamed Crabmeat and Egg Custard

PREPARATION TIME: 30 minutes

MICROWAVE COOKING TIME:
8-9 minutes

SERVES: 4 people

2 eggs, beaten
140ml/¼ pint/½ cup chicken stock
15ml/1 tbsp sherry
180g/6oz cooked crabmeat
4 chopped spring/green onions
3 chopped water chestnuts
2 finely chopped Chinese mushrooms,
*   pre-cooked 30 minutes*
15ml/1 tsp grated fresh ginger root
Salt

Mix the eggs, stock, sherry and add
the remaining ingredients. Spoon
into lightly oiled ramekins/custard
cups. Cover loosely and arrange in a

**Above: Barbecued Spare Ribs.
Right: Steamed Crabmeat and Egg
Custard.**

circle on the turntable and cook
1 minute on HIGH. Reduce to
LOW/DEFROST and cook for
7-8 minutes or until softly set.
Unmould onto plates and serve with
soy sauce. Surround with shredded
Chinese leaves/cabbage if desired.

Barbecued Spare Ribs

PREPARATION TIME: 10 minutes

MICROWAVE COOKING TIME:
20 minutes

SERVES: 4-6 people

1.35kg/3lbs pork spare ribs, cut up

MARINADE
60ml/2 fl oz/¼ cup dark soy sauce
45ml/3 tbsps hoisin sauce
5ml/1 tsp grated fresh ginger root
15ml/1 tbsp honey

Mix all the marinade ingredients in a large bowl and cook on HIGH for 1 minute. Add the ribs and mix to coat well. Cover and refrigerate for several hours, turning the ribs occasionally. Transfer the ribs to a shallow dish. Baste well with sauce and cover the dish with plastic wrap/cling film and cook on HIGH for 10 minutes, basting the ribs several times. Turn the ribs over and cook an additional 10 minutes on HIGH. Brush with any remaining marinade before serving. Garnish with cucumber twists if desired.

Stuffed Mushrooms with Pork and Water Chestnuts

PREPARATION TIME: 30 minutes

MICROWAVE COOKING TIME: 4 minutes per batch

SERVES: 4 people

12 dried Chinese mushrooms
120g/4oz minced/ground pork
2 water chestnuts, finely chopped
1 stick celery, finely chopped
10ml/2 tsps soy sauce
5ml/1 tsp oyster sauce
Salt and pepper

GARNISH
4 spring/green onions, sliced

Soak the mushrooms in hot water for 30 minutes. Mix all the remaining ingredients. Drain the mushrooms and reserve 120ml/4 fl oz/½ cup of the soaking water. Pat the mushrooms dry on paper towels and cut off the stems. Combine remaining ingredients and fill the mushrooms with the pork mixture, smoothing out with a knife. Place the mushrooms in 1 layer in a shallow dish, stuffing-side up. Pour around

This page: Stuffed Mushrooms with Pork and Water Chestnuts. Facing page: Garlic Prawns/Shrimp with Salt and Pepper (top) and Chili Prawns/Shrimp (bottom).

the soaking water and cover the dish with pierced plastic wrap/cling film. Cook on HIGH for 4 minutes. Baste occasionally with the mushroom liquid. Transfer the mushrooms to a serving dish and sprinkle with the onions. Serve hot.

Garlic Prawns/Shrimp with Salt and Pepper

PREPARATION TIME: 10-15 minutes

MICROWAVE COOKING TIME: 4½-5½ minutes

SERVES: 4 people

450g/1lb king prawns/jumbo shrimp
30ml/2 tbsps oil
2 cloves garlic, minced
45ml/3 tbsps oyster sauce
30ml/2 tbsps soy sauce
15ml/1 tbsp lemon juice

10ml/2 tsp coarsely ground black pepper
Salt

GARNISH
Spring/green onion brushes

Prepare the prawns/shrimp as for
Chili Prawns/Shrimp. Put the oil and
garlic into a bowl. Cover and cook
1 minute on HIGH. Add the oyster
sauce, soy sauce, lemon juice and
cook 30 seconds on HIGH. Stir in
the prawns/shrimp and cook for
3-4 minutes on MEDIUM. Sprinkle
with salt and pepper before serving.
Garnish with spring/green onion
brushes (see introduction).

Steamed Chicken Wontons

| **PREPARATION TIME:** 20 minutes |
| **MICROWAVE COOKING TIME:** 10 minutes per batch |
| **SERVES:** 4 people |

300g/10oz minced/ground chicken
2 chopped spring/green onions
2 chopped water chestnuts
Small piece ginger root, peeled and grated
30ml/2 tbsps light soy sauce
15ml/1 tbsp rice wine
15ml/1 tbsp sesame oil
1 egg, beaten
Pinch sugar
Salt and pepper
30 fresh wonton skins

Mince raw chicken in a food
processor and combine with the
remaining ingredients except the
wonton skins. Place a teaspoonful of
the mixture in the centre of each
wonton and twist the ends together
to seal. Brush lightly with water if the
ends won't stick together. Place
wontons in one layer in a casserole
dish and barely cover with water.
Cover with plastic wrap/cling film.
Cook in 2 batches for 2 minutes on
HIGH and 8 minutes on LOW/
DEFROST. Remove with a draining
spoon. Serve with Sweet and Sour
and Hot Mustard sauces.

Chili Prawns/Shrimp

| **PREPARATION TIME:** 10-15 minutes |
| **MICROWAVE COOKING TIME:** 4½-5½ minutes |
| **SERVES:** 4 people |

450g/1lb king prawns/jumbo shrimp
30ml/2 tbsps oil
2 cloves garlic, crushed
30ml/2 tbsps chili sauce (hot or sweet)
15ml/1 tbsp rice wine
15ml/1 tbsp lemon juice
Salt

GARNISH
Chili pepper flowers

Remove the heads and shells of the
prawns/shrimp, but leave on the very
ends of the tails. Wash, de-vein and
pat dry. Put the oil and garlic into a
bowl and cover with plastic wrap/
cling film. Cook on HIGH 1 minute.
Stir in the chili sauce, wine, lemon
juice and salt. Cook 30 seconds on
HIGH. Add the prawns/shrimp and
cook for 3-4 minutes on MEDIUM.
Serve hot or cold. Garnish with chili
pepper flowers (see introduction).

Steamed Barbecued Pork Dumplings

| **PREPARATION TIME:** 20 minutes |
| **MICROWAVE COOKING TIME:** 17-18 minutes per batch |
| **SERVES:** 4 people |

10ml/2 tsps oil
300g/10oz minced/ground pork
1 clove garlic, minced
Pinch sugar
30ml/2 tbsps soy sauce
30ml/2 tbsps cornflour/cornstarch mixed
  with 45ml/3 tbsps stock
120ml/4 fl oz/½ cup hoisin sauce
30 wonton skins

Combine oil, pork and garlic in a
casserole dish. Cover and cook on
HIGH 5 minutes, breaking up the
pork frequently with a fork as it
cooks. Mix the sugar, soy sauce,
cornflour/cornstarch and stock. Add
to the pork and cook a further 2-3
minutes until sauce thickens and
clears. Stir in the hoisin sauce. Fill
the wonton skins and pinch the
edges together, but leave some of the
filling exposed. Place in one layer in a
shallow dish, and barely cover with
water. Cover the dish with plastic
wrap/cling film and cook 2 minutes
on HIGH and 8 minutes on LOW/
DEFROST. Serve hot.

**Facing page: Steamed Chicken
Wontons (top) and Steamed
Barbecued Pork Dumplings
(bottom) – served with Sweet and
Sour and Hot Mustard Sauces.**

POULTRY

Singapore Chicken

PREPARATION TIME: 20 minutes

MICROWAVE COOKING TIME:
11 minutes plus 2 minutes
standing time

SERVES: 4 people

30ml/2 tbsps oil
10ml/2 tsps curry powder
450g/1lb chicken, skinned, boned and cut
    into bite-sized pieces
1 large onion, cut in large pieces
1 230g/8oz can pineapple pieces/chunks,
    juice reserved
1 300g/10oz can mandarin orange
    segments, juice reserved
15ml/1 tbsp cornflour/cornstarch
60g/2oz/1 cup bean sprouts
Dash soy sauce
Salt and pepper

Heat the oil in a large casserole dish
for 30 seconds on HIGH. Add the
curry powder, and cook 30 seconds
on HIGH. Add the chicken, cover
the dish and cook 5 minutes on
HIGH. Add the onion, mix the
cornflour/cornstarch with the
reserved pineapple and orange juice
and add to the chicken. Cover and
cook 5 minutes on HIGH, stirring
occasionally after 1 minute. When
the sauce thickens, add the
pineapple, orange segments and bean
sprouts. Leave to stand 2 minutes
before serving. Serve with fried or
plain boiled rice.

**This page: Sesame Chicken with
Garlic Sauce (top) and Lemon
Chicken (bottom). Facing page:
Singapore Chicken.**

Lemon Chicken

PREPARATION TIME: 30 minutes

MICROWAVE COOKING TIME:
7-9 minutes plus 2 minutes
standing time

SERVES: 4 people

4 chicken breasts, skinned, boned and cut
  into thin strips
60ml/4 tbsps soy sauce
10ml/2 tsps dry sherry or shao-hsing wine
Salt and pepper

SAUCE
45ml/3 tbsps salted black beans
30ml/2 tbsps water
90ml/6 tbsps lemon juice
280ml/8 fl oz/1 cup chicken stock
60ml/4 tbsps sugar
5ml/1 tsp sesame oil
30ml/3 tbsps cornflour/cornstarch
2 cloves garlic, finely minced
1.25ml/¼ tsp red pepper flakes

GARNISH
Lemon slices

Mix chicken with marinade
ingredients, cover and refrigerate
30 minutes. Crush the black beans,
combine with the water and leave to
stand until ready to use. Combine
remaining sauce ingredients in a
shallow dish. Add the chicken,
marinade and black beans, cover and
cook on HIGH for 7-9 minutes,
stirring halfway through the cooking
time. Once the cornflour/cornstarch
has cleared, leave the chicken to
stand, covered for 2 minutes before
serving. Garnish with lemon slices
and serve with rice.

Sesame Chicken with Garlic Sauce

PREPARATION TIME: 30 minutes

MICROWAVE COOKING TIME:
7-9 minutes plus 2 minutes
standing time

SERVES: 4 people

6 chicken thighs, skinned
15ml/1 tbsp sesame oil
4 cloves garlic, finely minced
5ml/1 tsp finely chopped ginger root
7.5ml/1½ tsp brown sugar
30ml/2 tbsps dark soy sauce
120ml/4 fl oz/½ cup chicken stock
2.5ml/½ tsp black pepper
10ml/2 tsps cornflour/cornstarch
6 spring/green onions, sliced
60ml/4 tbsps sesame seeds
Salt

Bone the chicken thighs and cut the
meat into thin strips or small pieces.
Combine the garlic, sesame oil,
ginger root, sugar, soy sauce and
pepper and pour over the chicken in
a shallow dish. Cover and refrigerate
for 30 minutes. Mix the cornflour/
cornstarch and stock, add to the
chicken and marinade and stir well.
Cover the dish and cook on HIGH
for 4-9 minutes, stirring halfway
through the cooking time. Add the
sesame seeds and onions and leave to
stand, covered, 2 minutes before
serving. Serve with rice or Chinese
noodles.

Chicken with Pea Pods

PREPARATION TIME: 20 minutes

MICROWAVE COOKING TIME:
8½-9½ minutes plus 2 minutes
standing time

SERVES: 4 people

30ml/2 tbsps oil
450g/1lb chicken breasts, skinned, boned
  and cut into thin slivers
10ml/2 tsps cornflour/cornstarch
45ml/3 tbsps rice wine
45ml/3 tbsps light soy sauce
30ml/2 tbsps oyster sauce
60ml/4 tbsps chicken stock
120g/4oz pea pods/mangetout
Dash sesame oil
Salt and pepper

Heat the oil 30 seconds on HIGH in
a large casserole dish. Mix the
remaining ingredients except the pea
pods/mangetout and pour over the
chicken. Cover and cook 7-9 minutes
on HIGH, stirring halfway through
the cooking time. Add the pea pods/
mangetout, re-cover the dish and

cook 30 seconds on HIGH. Leave to
stand for 2 minutes before serving.
Serve with rice.

Chicken with Hoisin Sauce and Cashews

PREPARATION TIME: 20 minutes

MICROWAVE COOKING TIME:
7-9 minutes plus 2 minutes
standing time

SERVES: 4 people

450g/1lb chicken, skinned, boned and cut
  into bite-sized pieces
15ml/1 tbsp cornflour/cornstarch
280ml/½ pint/1 cup stock
15ml/1 tbsp light soy sauce
1 clove garlic, finely minced
15ml/1 tbsp white wine
60ml/4 tbsps hoisin sauce
60g/2oz/½ cup roasted cashew nuts
4 spring/green onions, diagonally sliced

Combine the chicken with all the
ingredients except the nuts and
onions. Put into a casserole dish,
cover and cook on HIGH for 7-9
minutes, stirring halfway through the
cooking time. Once the sauce has
thickened and the cornflour/
cornstarch has cleared, add the nuts
and the spring/green onions.
Re-cover the dish and leave to stand
2 minutes before serving. Serve with
rice.

**Facing page: Chicken with
Peapods (top) and Chicken with
Hoisin Sauce and Cashews
(bottom).**

and salt if needed. Cook 30 seconds on HIGH, add bamboo shoots and leave to stand, covered, 2 minutes before serving. Serve with fried or plain boiled rice.

Lacquered Duck with Plum Sauce

PREPARATION TIME: 25 minutes

MICROWAVE COOKING TIME: 43-48 minutes plus 10 minutes standing time

SERVES: 4 people

SAUCE
See Plum Sauce recipe

GLAZE
60ml/4 tbsps/¼ cup honey
60ml/4 tbsps soy sauce

2.5kg/5lb duckling

GARNISH
60g/2oz/¼ cup toasted, chopped almonds
Spring/green onion brushes (see Introduction)

Brush the duckling with the honey and soy sauce glaze. Cook on rack on HIGH for 10 minutes. Turn over, brush with the glaze and cook 10 minutes on HIGH. Turn again and brush with some of the plum sauce. Lower the setting to MEDIUM and cook 15-30 minutes or until tender. Cover and leave to stand 10 minutes before cutting into 8 pieces with a cleaver or poultry shears. Pour over remaining plum sauce and sprinkle over the almonds. Garnish with onion brushes and serve with rice.

Diced Chicken and Peppers

PREPARATION TIME: 20 minutes

MICROWAVE COOKING TIME: 8½-10½ minutes plus 2 minutes standing time

SERVES: 4 people

30ml/2 tbsps oil
1 clove garlic, minced
450g/1lb chicken, skinned, boned and diced
2 green peppers, diced
1 small red chili pepper, diced
½ small can bamboo shoots, diced

5ml/1 tsp cornflour/cornstarch
30ml/2 tbsps white wine
30ml/2 tbsp soy sauce
60ml/4 tbsps chicken stock
Pinch sugar (optional)
Salt

Heat oil 30 seconds on HIGH in a large casserole dish. Add the garlic and cook 30 seconds on HIGH. Add the chicken and stir to coat with oil. Add the chili pepper, cornflour/cornstarch, wine, soy sauce and stock. Stir well and cover the dish. Cook 7-9 minutes on HIGH, stirring halfway through the cooking time. Add the green pepper, sugar (if using)

This page: Diced Chicken and Peppers. Facing page: Lacquered Duck with Plum Sauce.

Empress Chicken

PREPARATION TIME: 30 minutes

MICROWAVE COOKING TIME:
15 minutes plus 3 minutes
standing time

SERVES: 4 people

4 chicken wings
4 chicken breasts, skinned
12 dried Chinese mushrooms
120ml/4 fl oz/½ cup soy sauce
570ml/1 pint/2 cups chicken stock
    mixed with 45ml/3 tbsps cornflour/
    cornstarch
15ml/1 tbsp sugar
2 pieces star anise
2 slices ginger root
15ml/1 tbsp rice wine
2.5ml/½ tsp salt
2 cans bamboo shoots, drained and cut in
    strips if thick
4 spring/green onions, sliced

With a heavy cleaver, chop the chicken, through the bones, into large chunks. Remove any splinters of bone. Soak the mushrooms in hot water for 30 minutes. Drain and trim off the stems. Put the chicken, mushrooms and remaining ingredients, except the onions and bamboo shoots, into a deep casserole. Cover well and cook 15 minutes on HIGH or until the chicken is completely cooked. Add the bamboo shoots and sliced onions. Leave to stand 3 minutes and remove star anise before serving.

Golden Chicken with Walnuts

PREPARATION TIME: 20 minutes

MICROWAVE COOKING TIME:
7-9 minutes plus 2 minutes
standing time

SERVES: 4 people

450g/1lb chicken, skinned, boned and cut
    into bite-sized pieces
15ml/1 tbsp cornflour/cornstarch
15ml/1 tbsp light soy sauce
15ml/1 tbsp sherry
280ml/½ pint/1 cup stock

1 small can salted yellow beans
90g/3oz/¾ cup walnuts, roughly
    chopped
½ small can sliced bamboo shoots

Combine chicken, cornflour/cornstarch, soy sauce, sherry, stock, and yellow beans in a casserole dish. Cover and cook on HIGH for 7-9 minutes, stirring halfway through the cooking time. Once the sauce has thickened, add the walnuts and bamboo shoots. Leave to stand 2 minutes before serving.

Duck with Pineapple

PREPARATION TIME: 20 minutes

MICROWAVE COOKING TIME:
9-10 minutes

SERVES: 4 people

SAUCE
See Pineapple Sauce recipe

2.5kg/5lb duckling
30ml/2 tbsps oil
30ml/2 tbsps soy sauce

GARNISH
4 chives, shredded

Skin the duck and remove the leg and breast meat. Cut into thin slivers. Heat a browning dish 5 minutes on HIGH. Toss the oil and duck together, and add to the browning dish. Cook, uncovered, 4 minutes on HIGH. Add the soy sauce, cover the dish and reduce the setting to MEDIUM. Cook a further 3 minutes or until duck is tender. Remove duck to a serving dish and keep warm. Coat with the pineapple sauce and sprinkle on the chives. Serve with rice.

Duck with Five Spices

PREPARATION TIME: 20 minutes

MICROWAVE COOKING TIME:
30 minutes

SERVES: 4 people

2.5kg/5lb duckling
140ml/¼ pint/½ cup rice wine
140ml/¼ pint/½ cup light soy sauce
30ml/2 tbsps honey
1 clove garlic, finely minced
15ml/1 tbsp five-spice powder
60ml/4 tbsps chicken stock
30ml/2 tbsps cornflour/cornstarch,
    dissolved in 45ml/3 tbsps water

Remove the meat from the legs and breast of the duck. Take off the skin and cut the meat into bite-sized pieces. Combine with the remaining ingredients, except the cornflour/cornstarch and water, in a casserole. Cover the dish and cook on HIGH for 10 minutes. Reduce the setting and cook an additional 20 minutes on MEDIUM. Check the level of liquid from time to time and add more stock or water if necessary. When the duck is cooked, add a few spoonfuls of the cooking liquid to the cornflour/cornstarch and water. Return the mixture to the casserole and cook on HIGH for 2-3 minutes to thicken the sauce. Serve with rice or stir-fried vegetables. Garnish with Chinese parsley if desired.

Duck with Onions

PREPARATION TIME: 20 minutes

MICROWAVE COOKING TIME:
42-58 minutes plus 10 minutes
standing time

SERVES: 4 people

2.5kg/5lb duck
90ml/3 fl oz/⅓ cup soy sauce
2 pieces fresh ginger root, peeled and
    grated
45ml/3 tbsps white wine

**Facing page: Empress Chicken
(top) and Golden Chicken with
Walnuts (bottom).**

15ml/1 tbsp sugar
30ml/2 tbsps cornflour/cornstarch
   dissolved in 30ml/2 tbsps water
10 spring/green onions
1 small can sliced bamboo shoots
4 Chinese mushrooms, soaked and sliced
Salt

Combine the soy sauce and grated
ginger and brush over the breast side
of the duck. Place the duck on a rack
and cook for 10 minutes on HIGH.
Turn over, brush with the soy sauce
and cook 10 minutes on HIGH. Place

in a very large casserole or bowl. Add
3 spring/green onions, wine and
280ml/½ pint/1 cup water. Cover
the bowl or casserole and cook 15-30
minutes or until tender. Remove the
duck and keep warm. Discard the
cooked onions. Skim off fat from the
cooking liquid and mix a spoonful of
the liquid with the cornflour/
cornstarch and water and the sugar.
Add the bamboo shoots, mushrooms
and remaining onions, sliced, to the
sauce. Cook for 2-3 minutes on
HIGH until thick and clear. Cut the

duck into 8 pieces and pour over the
sauce to serve.

**This page: Duck with Pineapple.
Facing page: Duck with Five
Spices (top) and Duck with
Onions (bottom).**

MEAT DISHES

Szechuan Beef

PREPARATION TIME: 20 minutes

MICROWAVE COOKING TIME:
6-18 minutes

SERVES: 4 people

450g/1lb rump steak, shredded
30ml/2 tbsp oil
½ dried chili pepper, crushed
60ml/4 tbsps soy sauce
120ml/4 fl oz/½ cup stock
30ml/2 tbsps cornflour/cornstarch
3 sticks celery, shredded
1 sweet red pepper, shredded

Heat a browning dish for 5 minutes on HIGH. Combine meat and oil and add to the dish. Cook 2 minutes on HIGH in 2 or 3 batches. Re-heat browning dish 2 minutes after each batch. Add the crushed chili pepper. Mix the soy sauce and stock and gradually stir into the cornflour/cornstarch. Pour over the steak and cook 2-3 minutes. Add the celery and red pepper and mix together with the meat and sauce. Cook a further 1 minute on HIGH until the sauce has thickened but the vegetables are still crisp.

Beef with Broccoli

PREPARATION TIME: 20 minutes

MICROWAVE COOKING TIME:
7-8 minutes

SERVES: 4 people

450g/1lb rump steak, cut in thin strips
45ml/3 tbsps oil
60ml/2 fl oz/¼ cup soy sauce
15ml/1 tbsp cornflour/cornstarch

15ml/1 tbsp sherry
5ml/1 tsp sugar
90ml/3 fl oz/⅓ cup stock
½ bunch broccoli
10ml/2 tsps grated ginger root
Salt and pepper

Heat a browning dish 5 minutes on HIGH. Mix the beef and oil and add to the dish. Cook 2 minutes on HIGH in 2 or 3 batches. Slice the stalks of the broccoli thinly on the diagonal. Separate the flowerets into small pieces. Toss in the oil with the

This page: Beef with Broccoli. Facing page: Peking Sweet Lamb (top) and Szechuan Beef (bottom).

meat and cook for 1 minute on HIGH. Leave to stand covered while preparing the sauce. Mix the soy sauce, cornflour/cornstarch, sherry, sugar and ginger root in a small bowl. Cook 2-3 minutes on HIGH, until

thickened. Stir several times after 1 minute's cooking. Pour over the beef and broccoli. Cook a further 1 minute on HIGH. Adjust the seasoning and serve immediately with rice or noodles.

Beef with Tree Ears

PREPARATION TIME: 30 minutes

MICROWAVE COOKING TIME: 7-8 minutes

SERVES: 4 people

8 pieces dried black fungi (tree or wood ears)
450g/1lb rump steak, cut in thin strips
45ml/3 tbsps oil
60ml/4 tbsps soy sauce
15ml/1 tbsp rice wine
10ml/2 tsps chili sauce (sweet or hot)
90ml/3 fl oz/⅓ cup stock
15ml/1 tbsp cornflour/cornstarch
1 small bunch chives, chopped

Soak the tree ears for 20 minutes in hot water. Heat a browning dish for 5 minutes on HIGH. Combine oil and meat and add to the dish. Cook 2 minutes on HIGH in 2 or 3 batches. Re-heat dish 2 minutes after each batch. Drain the tree ears well and add whole to the steak in the browning dish. Cook 1 minute on HIGH, turning once. Mix the remaining ingredients, except the chives, together and pour over the meat and tree ears. Cook 2-3 minutes on HIGH, until the sauce thickens and clears. Sprinkle over the chopped chives before serving.

Peking Sweet Lamb

PREPARATION TIME: 1 hour

MICROWAVE COOKING TIME: 8-9 minutes plus 2 minutes standing time

SERVES: 4 people

450g/1lb lamb fillet or meat from the leg, thinly sliced
30ml/2 tbsps hoisin sauce
15ml/1 tbsp rice wine
15ml/1 tbsp sesame oil
30ml/2 tbsps sugar
30ml/2 tbsps light soy sauce
30ml/2 tbsps vinegar
15ml/1 tbsp rice wine
15ml/1 tbsp cornflour/cornstarch
140ml/¼ pint/½ cup plus 1 tbsp brown stock
5ml/1 tsp grated fresh ginger root

GARNISH
4 spring/green onions, diagonally sliced

Mix the lamb, hoisin sauce and 15ml/1 tbsp rice wine. Set aside for 1 hour. Combine the sesame oil and sugar in a casserole dish. Heat for 1 minute on HIGH and stir. Add the lamb to the casserole, cover and cook 2 minutes on HIGH. Lower the setting to MEDIUM. Mix the remaining ingredients together, except for the garnish, and pour over the lamb. Cook for 5-7 minutes more, or until lamb is tender. Leave to stand for 2 minutes before serving, garnished with the sliced spring/green onions.

Steamed Beef Balls with Two Different Mushrooms

PREPARATION TIME: 30 minutes

MICROWAVE COOKING TIME: 11-14 minutes

SERVES: 4-6 people

20 dried Chinese mushrooms
340g/12oz minced/ground beef
45ml/3 tbsps light soy sauce
10ml/2 tsps dry sherry
10ml/2 tsps grated fresh ginger root
Salt and pepper
24 fresh or frozen shelled peas
340-400g/12-14oz Chinese straw mushrooms or small button mushrooms
30ml/2 tbsps cornflour/cornstarch dissolved in 45ml/3 tbsps water

Soak the dried mushrooms for 30 minutes in hot water. Combine the ground/minced beef, half the soy sauce, sherry, ginger, salt and pepper and shape into 24 small balls. Press one pea into the top of each beef ball. Arrange in a glass dish with space between each ball if possible. Combine the remaining soy sauce

with 280ml/½ pint/1 cup water. Pour over the beef balls and cover loosely with plastic wrap/cling film. Cook on HIGH for 8-10 minutes. Turn the beef balls over and rearrange them once or twice during cooking. Make sure that those in the centre are brought to the outside of the dish. When the beef balls are cooked, remove to a serving dish and keep warm. Arrange in rows or in a circle, pea-side up. Skim the fat from the top of the cooking liquid. Combine the cornflour/cornstarch with a spoonful of liquid. Stir into the remaining liquid in the dish and mix well. Cook for 2-3 minutes on HIGH, stirring after 1 minute. Add the two different mushrooms and cook until the sauce thickens. Arrange the mushrooms on the serving dish, keeping the two different kinds separate. Pour over the sauce to serve.

Pink and Silver Pork

PREPARATION TIME: 15 minutes

MICROWAVE COOKING TIME: 11-16 minutes

SERVES: 4 people

225g/8oz pork fillet/tenderloin, cut into thin shreds
225g/8oz ham, cut into thin strips
280ml/½ pint/1 cup light stock
60ml/4 tbsps rice wine
30ml/2 tbsps light soy sauce
1 clove garlic, finely minced
1 small piece fresh ginger root, grated
15ml/1 tbsp cornflour/cornstarch mixed with 30ml/2 tbsps water
120g/4oz bean sprouts

Combine all the ingredients, except the bean sprouts, in a large casserole dish and cover. Cook for 10-15

Facing page: **Steamed Beef Balls with Two Different Mushrooms (top) and Beef with Tree Ears (bottom).**

53

minutes on MEDIUM, stirring halfway through the cooking time. Add the bean sprouts and cook a further 1 minute on HIGH. Leave to stand 2 minutes before serving.

Pork Chops, Shanghai Style

PREPARATION TIME: 15 minutes

MICROWAVE COOKING TIME: 14 minutes

SERVES: 4 people

90ml/⅓ cup soy sauce
30ml/1 tbsp brown sugar
30ml/1 tbsp oil
8 thin pork chops
1 onion, thinly sliced
10ml/2 tsps cornflour/cornstarch mixed with 10ml/2 tsps water

Mix the soy sauce and sugar with 120ml/4 fl oz/½ cup water. Heat a browning dish 5 minutes on HIGH. Pour in the oil and brown the pork on both sides about 2 minutes on HIGH. Brown in two batches if necessary. Remove the pork and add the onions. Cook to brown and soften slightly. Remove the onions from the browning dish and set aside. Return the pork chops to the dish and pour over the soy sauce mixture. Cover and cook a further 5 minutes on HIGH, or until the pork is tender. Remove the pork and keep warm. Mix the cornflour/cornstarch and water with the soy sauce mixture. Stir well and cook 1 minute on HIGH to thicken slightly. Add the onions and cook a further 1 minute on HIGH. Pour over the pork to serve. Serve with stir-fried vegetables. Garnish with Chinese parsley leaves if desired.

Kung-Pao Lamb

PREPARATION TIME: 20 minutes

MICROWAVE COOKING TIME: 10½-11½ minutes

SERVES: 4 people

450g/1lb lamb fillet or meat from the leg, thinly sliced
30ml/2 tbsps oil
1 clove garlic, finely minced
1 small piece fresh ginger root, grated
½ red chili pepper, finely chopped
60ml/4 tbsps soy sauce
120ml/4 fl oz/½ cup stock
30ml/2 tbsps white wine
5ml/1 tsp vinegar
5ml/1 tsp sugar
15ml/1 tbsp cornflour/cornstarch
1 small red pepper, cut in small dice
1 small green pepper, cut in small dice
4 spring/green onions, sliced
60g/2oz/½ cup roasted peanuts
Dash sesame oil

Heat a browning dish for 5 minutes on HIGH. Combine oil and lamb and add to the dish. Cook for about 2 minutes, turning often. Cook in

This page: Kung Pao Lamb. Facing page: Pork Chops, Shanghai Style (top) and Lion's Head (bottom).

two batches if necessary. Add the garlic, ginger and chili pepper and cook a further 2 minutes on HIGH. Mix the soy sauce, stock, wine, vinegar, sugar and cornflour/cornstarch together and add to the meat. Cover the browning dish or transfer the ingredients to a covered casserole dish. Cook on MEDIUM a further 4-6 minutes or until the lamb is tender. Add the diced peppers and cook a further 1 minute on HIGH. Stir in the sesame oil, peanuts and the spring/green onions. Heat 30 seconds on HIGH. Serve with rice.

Pork in Plum Sauce with Almonds

PREPARATION TIME: 30 minutes

MICROWAVE COOKING TIME: 11-18 minutes

SERVES: 4 people

SAUCE
Plum Sauce recipe
1 purple or red plum, thinly sliced

450g/1lb pork fillet/tenderloin, cut in thin slices
30ml/2 tbsps oil
30ml/2 tbsps soy sauce

GARNISH
60g/2oz/½ cup toasted whole almonds

When the plum sauce is ready, add the thinly sliced plum, keep the bowl covered and set aside while preparing the pork. Heat a browning dish for 5 minutes on HIGH. Pour in the oil and add the pork. Cook for 2 minutes on HIGH, stirring often. Add the soy sauce, cover the dish and cook for 5-7 minutes more on MEDIUM. When the pork is tender, pour over the plum sauce and heat for 1 minute on HIGH. Serve sprinkled with the toasted almonds.

Lion's Head

PREPARATION TIME: 20 minutes

MICROWAVE COOKING TIME: 19-20 minutes

SERVES: 4-6 people

900g/2lbs minced/ground pork
90ml/3 fl oz/⅓ cup soy sauce
10ml/2 tsps dry sherry
5ml/1 tsp brown sugar
60g/2oz/¼ cup cornflour/cornstarch
30ml/2 tbsps oil
5ml/1 tsp granulated sugar
25ml/1½ tbsps soy sauce
1 head Chinese leaves/cabbage
Salt (if necessary)

Mix pork, 90ml/3 fl oz/⅓ cup soy sauce, sherry, brown sugar, 15ml/ 1 tbsp cornflour/cornstarch and shape into 5cm/2 inch balls. Heat a

browning dish 5 minutes on HIGH. Add the oil and the pork balls. Brown the pork balls 3-5 minutes on HIGH, turning often. Cook in 2 batches, re-heating the dish in between each batch. If the browning dish has a cover, leave the pork balls in it or transfer to a large casserole. Add the granulated sugar, remaining soy sauce and 280ml/½ pint/1 cup water. Cover and cook 9 minutes on HIGH. Turn the pork balls often and rearrange to bring those in the middle of the dish to the outside. Shred the Chinese leaves/cabbage finely and add it to the casserole with the pork balls. Cook 1 minute on

This page: Pink and Silver Pork (top) and Pork in Plum Sauce with Almonds (bottom). Facing page: Jade and Ivory Pork.

HIGH. Remove the pork and Chinese leaves/cabbage to a serving dish and keep warm. Mix the remaining cornflour/cornstarch with 30ml/2 tbsps water and add to the cooking liquid from the pork balls. Cook 2-3 minutes, uncovered, on HIGH or until the sauce has thickened. Arrange the cabbage on a serving dish with the pork balls on top. Pour over the sauce to serve.

Jade and Ivory Pork

PREPARATION TIME: 30 minutes

MICROWAVE COOKING TIME:
10-12 minutes

SERVES: 4 people

450g/1lb pork fillet/tenderloin, cut in
*   very fine strips*
45ml/3 tbsps oil
45ml/3 tbsps yellow beans
60ml/4 tbsps light soy sauce
30ml/2 tbsps rice wine
15ml/1 tbsp cornflour/cornstarch
180ml/6 fl oz/¾ cup chicken stock
225g/8oz can bamboo shoots, cut in
*   strips if necessary*
1 large green pepper, cut in strips about the
*   same size as bamboo shoots*

Heat a browning dish for 5 minutes
on HIGH. Mix meat and oil and add
to the dish. Cook for 2 minutes on
HIGH, stirring often. Combine the
yellow beans, soy sauce, wine,
cornflour/cornstarch and stock. Mix
very well and pour over the pork.
Cover the dish or transfer to a
covered casserole and cook for
5-7 minutes on MEDIUM, stirring
halfway through the cooking time.
Cook on HIGH for 2 minutes until
thickened. Add the pepper and
bamboo shoots and cook a further
1 minute on HIGH. Serve with rice
or noodles.

Beef with Green Pepper, Tomato and Black Beans

PREPARATION TIME: 30 minutes

MICROWAVE COOKING TIME:
8-10 minutes

SERVES: 4 people

450g/1lb rump steak, cut in thin slices
60ml/4 tbsps soy sauce
10ml/2 tsps dry sherry or rice wine

SAUCE
45ml/3 tbsps salted black beans
30ml/2 tbsps water
280ml/8 fl oz/1 cup brown stock
15ml/1 tbsp sugar

30ml/3 tbsps cornflour/cornstarch
*   dissolved in the stock*
1 clove garlic, finely minced
1 large green pepper, cut in 2.5cm/1 inch
*   pieces*
3 tomatoes, peeled and quartered
Salt and pepper

Mix the steak, soy sauce and wine
and leave to marinate, covered, in the
refrigerator for 30 minutes. Crush
the black beans and mix with the
water. Leave to stand until ready to
use. Combine all the ingredients in a
shallow dish, except for the pepper
and tomatoes. Cover the dish and
cook on HIGH for 7-9 minutes,

**This page: Beef with Green
Pepper, Tomato and Black Beans.
Facing page: Prawns/Shrimp with
Pea Pods and Sweetcorn.**

stirring halfway through the cooking
time. Once the sauce has cleared, add
the pepper and tomatoes and cook
1 minute further on HIGH. Serve
with rice. Garnish with spring/green
onion brushes if desired.

Microwave
CHINESE COOKING

FISH AND SEAFOOD

Prawns/Shrimp with Pea Pods and Sweetcorn

PREPARATION TIME: 20 minutes

MICROWAVE COOKING TIME:
5-8 minutes

SERVES: 4 people

675g/1½ lbs shelled king prawns/jumbo
shrimp, uncooked
45ml/3 tbsps oil
1 clove garlic, minced
1 small piece ginger root, minced
60ml/4 tbsps light stock
60ml/4 tbsps light soy sauce
60ml/4 tbsps rice wine
10ml/2 tsps cornflour/cornstarch
30ml/2 tbsps Chinese parsley
60g/2 oz pea pods/mangetout
120g/4oz baby ears of corn
Salt

Heat a browning dish for 5 minutes on HIGH. Shell and de-vein the prawns/shrimp if necessary. Add the oil to the dish and the prawns/ shrimp. Add the garlic and ginger and cook for 1-2 minutes on HIGH, stirring often. Combine the stock, soy sauce, wine and cornflour/ cornstarch. Pour over the prawns/ shrimp and cook for 3-4 minutes on MEDIUM, stirring halfway through the cooking time. Cut the stalks off the pea pods/mangetout and add with the ears of corn to the dish. Cut the corn in half lengthwise if the ears are large. Cook for 1-2 minutes on MEDIUM, until the sauce thickens and clears. If the prawns/ shrimp are cooked after 3-4 minutes, remove them before adding the vegetables. Serve with rice or noodles.

Sweet and Sour Prawns/ Shrimp

PREPARATION TIME: 20 minutes

MICROWAVE COOKING TIME:
4-5 minutes plus 2 minutes
standing time

SERVES: 4 people

SAUCE
Double recipe Sweet and Sour Sauce.
Use reserved pineapple juice made up to
*   570ml/1 pint/2 cups with more*
*   canned juice.*

1 large green pepper, cut in 2.5cm/
*   1 inch pieces*
4 tomatoes, peeled and quartered
4 spring/green onions, cut in 2.5cm/
*   1 inch pieces*
225g/8oz can pineapple pieces/chunks,
*   juice reserved*
675g/1½ lbs shelled prawns/shrimp,
*   de-veined*

Prepare the Sweet and Sour Sauce.
Add the green pepper to the hot
sauce and cook 1 minute on HIGH.
Add the pineapple, tomatoes, onions,
prawns/shrimp and cover tightly.
Leave to stand 3 minutes before
serving. Serve with rice.

Embroidered Crabmeat Balls

PREPARATION TIME: 25 minutes

MICROWAVE COOKING TIME:
5-6 minutes

SERVES: 4-6 people

450g/1lb crabmeat
2-3 egg whites
5ml/1 tsp salt
Pinch pepper
15ml/1 tbsp sherry
15ml/1 tbsp cornflour/cornstarch
½ green pepper, finely chopped
¼ red pepper, finely chopped
30ml/2 tbsps finely chopped ham
2 spring/green onions, finely chopped
3 large leaves Chinese leaves/cabbage,
*   chopped*
2.5ml/½ tsp ground ginger
280ml/½ pint/1 cup hot chicken stock

30ml/2 tbsps cornflour/cornstarch
30ml/2 tbsps light soy sauce
Dash sesame oil

Mix the first 11 ingredients, adding
only 2 egg whites. If the mixture is
dry and crumbly, add some of the
remaining white until the mixture
will hold together. Shape into 2.5cm/
1 inch balls. The balls should not be
smooth. Place in a single layer in a
large, shallow dish. Pour around the
hot stock and cover the dish. Cook
3 minutes on HIGH, rearranging the
balls once during cooking to bring
the ones in the centre of the dish to
the outside. Remove the balls and
keep warm. Mix the remaining
cornflour/cornstarch with the soy
sauce in a glass measure and
gradually add the stock. Stir well and
cook 2-3 minutes on HIGH, until
thickened. Add the sesame oil and
pour over the crabmeat balls to
serve.

Scallops in Pepper Sauce

PREPARATION TIME: 20 minutes

MICROWAVE COOKING TIME:
13-15 minutes

SERVES: 4 people

450g/1lb scallops, shelled and cleaned,
*   roe attached if possible*
½ clove garlic, finely chopped
45ml/3 tbsps rice wine
45ml/3 tbsps light soy sauce
15ml/1 tbsp cornflour/cornstarch
*   dissolved in 90ml/3 fl oz/⅓ cup light*
*   stock*
60ml/4 tbsps sweet chili sauce
1 small piece fresh ginger root, peeled and
*   chopped*
1 green pepper, thinly sliced
4 spring/green onions, sliced or shredded
Pinch sugar
Salt and pepper

If the scallops are large, cut in half,
horizontally. Place in a casserole dish
with the garlic, wine, soy sauce, sugar
and salt and pepper. Cover the dish
and cook for 10 minutes on
MEDIUM. Remove the scallops
and keep warm. Add the cornflou

cornstarch and stock to the hot
cooking liquid and stir well. Add the
chili sauce and ginger root and cook
2-3 minutes, or until thickened.
Add the green pepper and onions to
the sauce and return the scallops
to the dish. Cook 1-2 minutes on
HIGH, until the scallops are cooked
and the vegetables are still crisp.
Serve with rice.

Pineapple Prawns/Shrimp with Peppers

PREPARATION TIME: 20 minutes

MICROWAVE COOKING TIME:
6-7 minutes

SERVES: 4 people

SAUCE
Pineapple Sauce recipe with
30ml/2 tbsps rice wine
30ml/2 tbsps light soy sauce
1 large green pepper, cut in thin strips
675/1½ lbs shelled king prawns/jumbo
*   shrimp, de-veined*
45ml/3 tbsps oil

Add the rice wine and soy sauce to
the Pineapple Sauce recipe. If the
sauce is still too thick, thin with a
spoonful of water. Heat a browning
dish 5 minutes on HIGH. Pour in the
oil and add the prawns/shrimp.
Cook 1 minute on HIGH. Pour over
the sauce, add the strips of pepper
and cook 3 minutes on MEDIUM.
Do not overcook or prawns/shrimp
will toughen. Serve with rice.

120g/4oz/½ cup brown sugar
30g/2 tbsps cornflour/cornstarch
90ml/3 fl oz vinegar
30ml/2 tbsps light soy sauce
2 carrots, thinly sliced
1 clove garlic, minced
2 spring/green onions, sliced
Salt and pepper

Place the trout in a shallow dish with the sherry, ginger and enough water to just cover the fish. Cover the dish with pierced plastic wrap/cling film and cook 8-9 minutes on HIGH. Remove the fish to a serving dish and peel off the skin from one side. Cover and keep warm. Reserve the cooking liquid from the fish. Combine the remaining ingredients except the spring/green onions and carrots in a deep bowl. Cook for 2-3 minutes on HIGH or until the sauce thickens and clears. Thin down the sauce with some of the fish cooking liquid until of thick coating consistency. Add the carrots and onions and cook 1 minute on HIGH. Pour over some of the sauce to serve with the fish and serve the rest of the sauce separately.

Prawns/Shrimp with Peas

PREPARATION TIME: 15 minutes

MICROWAVE COOKING TIME:
3 minutes plus 2 minutes standing time

SERVES: 4 people

675g/1½ lbs shelled king prawns/jumbo
    shrimp
15ml/1 tbsp cornflour/cornstarch
30ml/2 tbsps rice wine
90ml/3 fl oz/⅓ cup light stock
30ml/2 tbsps light soy sauce
Dash sesame oil
120g/4oz/½ cup frozen peas

Shell and de-vein the prawns/shrimp and set aside. Combine the remaining ingredients, except the peas, in a deep bowl. Cook for 2-3 minutes on HIGH, or until the sauce thickens, stirring after 1 minute.

Add the prawns/shrimp, lower the setting to MEDIUM and cook for about 3 minutes. Check the prawns/shrimp after 2 minutes. They must not overcook or they will toughen. Add the frozen peas during the last 1 minute of cooking. Add salt if necessary and serve with rice or noodles.

Sweet and Sour Fish

PREPARATION TIME: 15 minutes

MICROWAVE COOKING TIME:
11-13 minutes

SERVES: 4 people

4 trout, cleaned and trimmed
30ml/2 tbsps sherry
1 small piece ginger root, peeled and sliced

Squid with Prawns/Shrimp and Tomatoes

PREPARATION TIME: 25 minutes

MICROWAVE COOKING TIME:
4-5 minutes

SERVES: 4 people

225g/8oz squid, cleaned
225g/8oz prawns/shrimp, peeled
30ml/2 tbsps oil

This page: Sweet and Sour Fish. Facing page: Pineapple Prawns/ Shrimp with Peppers (top) and Prawns/Shrimp with Peas (bottom).

SAUCE
180ml/6 fl oz/¾ cup stock
30ml/2 tbsps rice wine
15ml/1 tbsp soy sauce
30ml/2 tbsps tomato purée/paste
15ml/1 tbsp cornflour/cornstarch
1.25ml/¼ tsp ground ginger
Salt and pepper
4 tomatoes, peeled and sliced

Heat the oil in a casserole dish for 30 seconds on HIGH. Cut the squid into rings and add to the oil with the prawns/shrimp. Stir to coat and cook, covered, on MEDIUM for 2 minutes. Set aside. If using cooked prawns/shrimp, add to the squid after 2 minutes. Combine all the sauce ingredients, except the tomatoes. Cook for 2-3 minutes on HIGH or until sauce has thickened. Add the tomatoes and pour over the squid. Leave to stand a few minutes to reheat the seafood. Serve with rice.

Crystal Steamed Sea Bass

PREPARATION TIME: 30 minutes

MICROWAVE COOKING TIME: 16-18 minutes

SERVES: 4 people

1kg/2¼ lb sea bass, cleaned and trimmed
1 small piece fresh ginger root, thinly sliced
280ml/½ pint/1 cup white wine
280ml/½ pint/1 cup water
30ml/2 tbsps vegetable oil and sesame oil mixed
1-2 carrots, cut in very fine shreds
6 spring/green onions, cut in very fine shreds
5ml/1 tsp cornflour/cornstarch
30ml/2 tbsps light soy sauce
Salt

Sprinkle the fish lightly with salt and place in a large, shallow dish or into a cooking bag. Cover head and tail with foil. Put the slices of ginger root into the cavity and pour over the wine and water. Cover the dish or seal the bag. Cook 14-16 minutes on MEDIUM, removing foil for the last 4-6 minutes. Leave to stand while preparing the vegetables. Heat a browning dish for 4 minutes on

This page: Crystal Steamed Sea Bass. Facing page: Squid with Prawns/Shrimp and Tomatoes (top) and Embroidered Crabmeat Balls (bottom).

HIGH. Pour in the oil and add the carrots and onions. Cook, uncovered for 2 minutes on HIGH. Remove the fish to a serving dish. Strain the stock through muslin/cheesecloth to remove any sediment and add 5ml/ 1 tsp cornflour/cornstarch and cook 2-3 minutes on HIGH. Pour over the fish. Sprinkle on the soy sauce and swirl through the clear stock. Sprinkle or arrange the vegetables before serving. Garnish with a sprig of Chinese parsley.

Fish Steamed on Lotus Leaves

PREPARATION TIME: 25 minutes

MICROWAVE COOKING TIME: 13-16 minutes

SERVES: 4 people

4 small fish such as red mullet or small trout
4 dried Chinese mushrooms, soaked 30 minutes in hot water
45g/3 tbsps shrimp
30ml/2 tbsps oil
4 strips bacon/streaky bacon, diced
1 small piece fresh ginger root, slivered
4 spring/green onions, finely chopped
30ml/2 tbsps soy sauce
280ml/½ pint/1 cup stock
30ml/2 tbsps cornflour/cornstarch,

This page: Fish Steamed on Lotus Leaves. Facing page: Cantonese Lobster.

Cantonese Lobster

PREPARATION TIME: 30 minutes

MICROWAVE COOKING TIME:
5-6 minutes plus 1 minute
standing time

SERVES: 4 people

1 560-675g/1¼-1½ lb cooked lobster
10ml/2 tsps black beans soaked in 30ml/
   2 tbsps water
4-6 dried Chinese mushrooms, soaked
   30 minutes in hot water
10ml/2 tsps soy sauce
140ml/¼ pint/½ cup plus 2 tbsps light
   stock
60ml/4 tbsps rice wine
1 clove garlic, minced
25ml/1½ tbsps cornflour/cornstarch
   dissolved in 60ml/4 tbsps mushroom
   soaking liquid
45ml/3 tbsps chives
30g/1oz pea pods/mangetout
4 leaves Chinese leaves/cabbage, cut into
   2.5cm/1 inch strips
45g/1½ oz bean sprouts
5 water chestnuts, sliced
Salt and pepper

Combine the soy sauce, stock, wine
and cornflour/cornstarch. Cook in a
deep bowl for 2-3 minutes on HIGH,
or until the sauce thickens. If it is
too thick, add more of the
mushroom soaking liquid. Drain and
slice the Chinese mushrooms and
add to the sauce with the black
beans, slightly crushed. Remove the
tail and claw meat from the lobster
and as much of the leg meat as
possible. Cut the meat into 1.25cm/
½ inch pieces, leaving the claws
whole if desired. Add the vegetables
to the sauce and cook 2 minutes on
HIGH. Stir in the lobster and leave
covered for 1 minute before serving.
Use the whole claws without their
shells as garnish if desired.

Sesame Crab in Asparagus Ring

PREPARATION TIME: 20 minutes

MICROWAVE COOKING TIME:
9-10 minutes

SERVES: 4 people

dissolved in 60ml/4 tbsps of the
   mushroom liquid
Salt and pepper
Sliced lotus root or bamboo shoots, cut in
   thin strips
2-4 lotus leaves, depending on size

Trim off the fins of the fish and trim
the tails neatly. Set fish aside in the
refrigerator until ready to cook.
Heat a browning dish for 5 minutes
on HIGH. Pour in the oil and add the
bacon. Cook 1 minute until beginning
to brown. Drain the mushrooms and
the shrimp. Dice the mushrooms and
add to the bacon along with the
shrimp, onions and ginger. Cook a
further 1 minute on HIGH or until
bacon is crisp. Place 1 or 2 lotus
leaves in the bottom of a large,
shallow dish. Lay the fish on top and
scatter over the bacon mixture.
Cover the fish with the remaining
lotus leaves and pour over the soy
sauce and stock. Cover the dish and
cook the fish on HIGH for 9-11
minutes. When the fish are cooked,
remove them and the lotus leaves
from the dish and keep them warm.
Add the cornflour/cornstarch to the
fish cooking liquid and stir well.
Add salt and pepper and cook for
2-3 minutes on HIGH, or until the
sauce has thickened. Add the lotus
root or bamboo shoots. Remove the
top layer of lotus leaves and serve the
fish on the bottom leaves with the
sauce.

45ml/3 tbsps sesame paste (tahini)
30ml/2 tbsps light soy sauce
120ml/4 fl oz/½ cup light stock
30ml/2 tbsps sherry
15ml/1 tbsp cornflour/cornstarch
30ml/2 tbsps Szechwan peppercorns
30ml/2 tbsps oil
450g/1lb asparagus, fresh or frozen, cut
  on the diagonal into 5cm/2 inch pieces
30ml/2 tbsps Chinese parsley leaves,
  left whole
4 spring/green onions, thinly sliced
  or shredded
Salt
Pinch sugar (optional)

450g/1lb crabmeat (including some pink
  claw meat)
Sesame seeds

Combine the first 6 ingredients in
a deep bowl. Cook for 2-3 minutes
on HIGH, until thick, and set aside.
Heat a browning dish 5 minutes on
HIGH. Pour in the oil and add the
asparagus. Stir-fry on HIGH for
4 minutes. If further cooking is
needed, cover the dish and cook 1
minute on HIGH. Add the Chinese
parsley, spring/green onions and
crabmeat to the reserved sauce.

**This page: Sesame Crab in
Asparagus Ring. Facing page:
Kung Pao Prawns/Shrimp (top)
and Crabmeat Egg Foo Yung,
Cantonese (bottom).**

Reheat 1 minute on HIGH. Add salt
and sugar if desired. Arrange the
asparagus pieces in a ring on a
serving dish and pile the crabmeat
mixture into the centre. Sprinkle
with sesame seeds to serve.

30ml/2 heaped tbsps of the egg mixture at a time. Cook 2-4 patties at a time for 2-3 minutes on MEDIUM on the first side, turn over and cook 1-2 minutes on the other. Re-heat browning dish after each batch. Keep warm while making the sauce. Combine all the sauce ingredients in a deep bowl. Cook, uncovered, 2-3 minutes on HIGH or until the sauce thickens and clears. Pour over the Egg Foo Yung to serve.

Kung Pao Prawns/Shrimp

PREPARATION TIME: 20 minutes

MICROWAVE COOKING TIME:
5 minutes plus 2 minutes
standing time

SERVES: 4 people

*450g/1lb shelled king prawns/jumbo
   shrimp, de-veined*
5ml/1 tsp chopped fresh ginger root
5ml/1 tsp chopped garlic
Salt and pepper
1.25ml/¼ tsp sugar
1 small onion, coarsely chopped
*1 courgette/zucchini cut into 1.25cm/
   ½ inch cubes*
60g/2oz/½ cup roasted cashew nuts

SAUCE
15ml/1 tbsp cornflour/cornstarch
120ml/4 fl oz/½ cup stock
60ml/4 tbsps soy sauce
5ml/1 tsp red bean paste (optional)
5ml/1 tsp sesame oil
15ml/1 tbsp shao-hsing wine or rice wine

Combine the prawns/shrimp, ginger, garlic, sugar, salt and pepper in a casserole dish. Cover and refrigerate for 20 minutes. Combine all the sauce ingredients and pour over the prawns/shrimp. Cover and cook for 3 minutes on MEDIUM. Stir often and do not allow the prawns/shrimp to overcook. Add the remaining ingredients and cook 2 minutes on HIGH. Leave to stand 2 minutes before serving. Serve with rice.

Crabmeat Egg Foo Yung, Cantonese

PREPARATION TIME: 20 minutes

MICROWAVE COOKING TIME:
10-13 minutes

SERVES: 4 people

6 eggs
225g/8oz/1 cup crabmeat
2 sticks celery, thinly sliced
6 large mushrooms, thinly sliced
60g/2oz/1 cup bean sprouts
½ onion, thinly sliced
5ml/1 tsp sherry
Salt and pepper

30ml/2 tbsps oil

SAUCE
15ml/1 tbsp cornflour/cornstarch
5ml/1 tsp sugar
280ml/8 fl oz/1 cup chicken stock
10ml/2 tsp soy sauce
5ml/1 tsp sherry
5ml/1 tsp sesame oil
2.5ml/½ tsp ketchup
Salt

Heat a browning dish 5 minutes on HIGH. Beat the eggs and mix in the remaining ingredients except the oil and those for the sauce. Add oil to the browning dish and spoon in

Microwave
CHINESE COOKING

VEGETABLES

Spinach, Chinese Style

PREPARATION TIME: 15 minutes

MICROWAVE COOKING TIME:
2 minutes plus 1 minute
standing time

SERVES: 4 people

675g/1½ lbs fresh spinach, stalks removed
30ml/2 tbsps oil
Salt
Sugar
Soy sauce
2 spring/green onions, white part only,
*   finely sliced*

Wash the spinach well and pat the
leaves dry. Heat a browning dish for
4 minutes on HIGH. Pour in the oil
and add the spinach. Add a pinch of
salt and sugar and cook, uncovered,
for 2 minutes on HIGH, stirring
frequently. Add the spring/green
onions and a dash of soy sauce.
Leave to stand 1 minute before
serving.

Sweet-Sour Cabbage

PREPARATION TIME: 20 minutes

MICROWAVE COOKING TIME:
11-13 minutes

SERVES: 4 people

**This page: Spinach, Chinese Style
(top) and Spicy Cucumbers
(bottom). Facing page: Sweet-Sour
Cabbage.**

1 medium head white cabbage,
    about 900g/2lbs
1 small red chili pepper (use less if desired)
120g/4oz/½ cup light brown sugar
90ml/3 fl oz/⅓ cup rice vinegar
30ml/2 tbsps light soy sauce
Salt
45ml/3 tbsps oil

Cut the cabbage into 1.25cm/½ inch slices, discarding the core. Cut the chili pepper into thin, short strips, discarding the seeds. Mix all the ingredients together except the oil. Pour the oil into a large bowl and heat for 2 minutes on HIGH. Add the cabbage and the liquid and cover the bowl with pierced plastic wrap/cling film. Cook on HIGH for 9-11 minutes. Allow to cool in the bowl, stirring frequently. When cold, refrigerate. Keeps several days.

Ten Varieties of Beauty

PREPARATION TIME: 20 minutes

MICROWAVE COOKING TIME:
6-8 minutes

SERVES: 4-6 people

60ml/4 tbsps oil
3 sticks celery, diagonally sliced
2 carrots, peeled and cut into ribbons with
    a vegetable peeler
90g/3oz pea pods/mangetout
1 red pepper, thickly sliced
4 spring/green onions, diagonally sliced
8 ears of baby corn
60g/2oz bean sprouts
10 water chestnuts, sliced
½ small can sliced bamboo shoots
10 Chinese dried mushrooms, soaked in
    hot water, stalks removed
280ml/½ pint/1 cup chicken stock
30ml/2 tbsps cornflour/cornstarch
45ml/3 tbsps light soy sauce
Sesame oil

Heat a browning dish for 5 minutes on HIGH. Pour in the oil and add the celery and carrots. Cook for 1 minute on HIGH. Remove from the dish and add the pea pods/mangetout, red pepper and corn. Cook for 1 minute on HIGH and place with the celery

and carrots. Add the onions, bean sprouts, water chestnuts and bamboo shoots to the dish. Cook for 1 minute on HIGH, adding the mushrooms after 30 seconds. Place with the rest of vegetables. Combine the rest of the ingredients in a glass measure. Cook 2-3 minutes on HIGH until thickened. Taste and add salt if necessary. Pour over the vegetables and stir carefully. Reheat for 1-2 minutes on HIGH before serving.

Spicy Cucumbers

PREPARATION TIME: 30 minutes

MICROWAVE COOKING TIME:
2 minutes

SERVES: 4 people

1 large cucumber
Salt
45ml/3 tbsps light soy sauce
Pinch five-spice powder
1.25ml/¼ tsp crushed red pepper
10ml/2 tsp sesame oil
15ml/1 tbsp rice vinegar
45ml/3 tbsps Chinese parsley leaves

Peel thin strips off the cucumber for a white and green stripe effect. Cut in half lengthwise, or in quarters if the cucumber is thick. Cut the lengths into 5cm/2 inch pieces. Sprinkle with salt and leave to stand 30 minutes. Wash and dry well. Combine the cucumber with all the remaining ingredients except the parsley in a deep bowl. Partially cover and cook for 2 minutes on HIGH. Add the parsley and leave in the bowl to cool. When cold, refrigerate. Serve on the same day.

Beans with Tree Ears and Bamboo Shoots

PREPARATION TIME: 30 minutes

MICROWAVE COOKING TIME:
4 minutes

SERVES: 4 people

6 pieces Chinese black fungi (tree or
    wood ears), soaked 30 minutes
340g/8oz green/French beans, cut into
    5cm/2 inch diagonal pieces
2 whole pieces canned bamboo shoots,
    cut into thin triangular pieces
30ml/2 tbsps oil
30ml/2 tbsps soy sauce
10ml/2 tsps cornflour/cornstarch
60ml/4 tbsps light stock and wine mixed
Dash sesame oil
Salt and pepper

Heat a browning dish for 5 minutes on HIGH. Pour in the oil and add the beans and bamboo shoots. Cook, uncovered, for 2 minutes on HIGH. Add the tree ears, cover the dish and leave to stand while preparing the sauce. Mix the remaining ingredients except the sesame oil in a glass measure. Cook for 2 minutes on HIGH, stirring once until thickened. Combine with the vegetables and stir in the sesame oil to serve.

Pea Pods/Mangetout with Water Chestnuts

PREPARATION TIME: 15 minutes

MICROWAVE COOKING TIME:
4 minutes

SERVES: 4 people

225g/8oz pea pods/mangetout, stems
    trimmed off
30ml/2 tbsps oil
Pinch sugar
Pinch salt
1 small can water chestnuts, sliced in
    rounds

Facing page: Ten Varieties of Beauty.

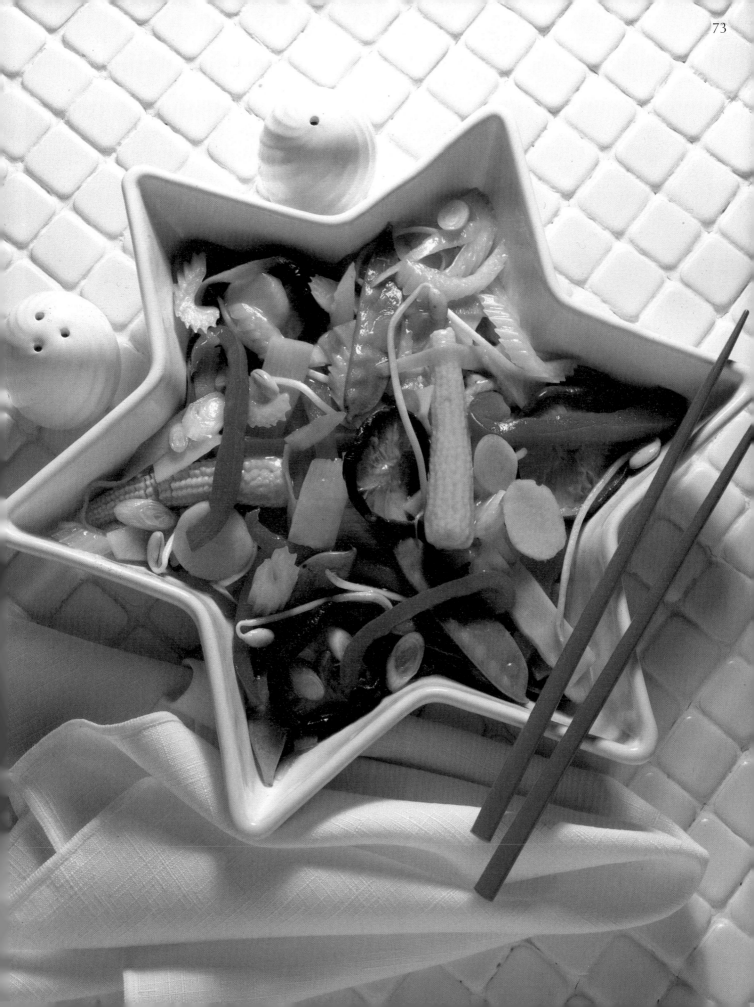

60ml/4 tbsps light stock
7.5ml/1½ tsps cornflour/cornstarch
Dash sesame oil

Heat a browning dish for 5 minutes on HIGH. Pour in the oil and add the pea pods/mangetout. Add the salt and sugar and cook 2 minutes on HIGH, stirring frequently. Add the water chestnuts, cover, and set aside while preparing the sauce. Combine the stock and cornflour/cornstarch in a glass measure. Cook for 2

This page: Pea Pods/Mangetout with Water Chestnuts. Facing page: Beans with Tree Ears and Bamboo Shoots.

minutes on HIGH, stirring once, until thickened. Add the sesame oil and mix with the vegetables to serve.

Asparagus Salad

PREPARATION TIME: 15 minutes

MICROWAVE COOKING TIME: 5-6 minutes

SERVES: 4 people

450g/1lb fresh asparagus
45ml/3 tbsps soy sauce
10ml/2 tsps sesame oil
15ml/1 tbsp sesame seeds

Trim the ends of the asparagus

the broccoli stems. Cut the flowerets from the stems in small clusters. Peel the stems with a vegetable peeler and cut them into thin diagonal slices. Pour the oil into the browning dish and add the broccoli stem slices. Add the ginger and cook, uncovered, for 2 minutes on HIGH, stirring frequently. Add the flowerets, cover and set aside while preparing the sauce. Combine the remaining ingredients in a glass measure. Cook, uncovered, for 5-6 minutes on HIGH until thickened. Pour over the broccoli and stir together to serve.

Steamed Aubergine/ Eggplant

PREPARATION TIME: 30 minutes

MICROWAVE COOKING TIME: 6-8 minutes

SERVES: 4 people

1 large or 2 small aubergines/eggplants
15ml/1 tbsp sesame oil
45ml/3 tbsps rice vinegar or white wine vinegar
45ml/3 tbsps light brown sugar
30ml/2 tbsps light soy sauce
15ml/1 tbsp fresh ginger root, grated
1 clove garlic, minced
Salt

Cut off the stems of the aubergines/ eggplants and then cut them in half, lengthwise. Lightly score the surface of each half and sprinkle with salt. Leave to stand for 30 minutes. Combine the remaining ingredients in a glass measure. Cook for 1 minute on HIGH to dissolve sugar. Stir well and set aside to allow flavours to blend. Wash the aubergines/ eggplants and dry well. Cut in quarters, lengthwise, and then into 2.5cm/1 inch wedges. Put into a casserole dish with 120ml/4 fl oz/ ½ cup water. Cover and cook 5-7 minutes or until just tender. Stir several times during cooking. Drain well. Pour over the sauce and serve hot or cold.

This page: Ginger Broccoli. Facing page: Asparagus Salad (top) and Steamed Aubergine/Eggplant (bottom).

spears, wash and drain well. Cut on the diagonal into 3.75cm/1½ inch lengths, leaving the tips whole. Put into a casserole dish with 120ml/ 4 fl oz/½ cup water. Cook, covered, for 5-6 minutes on HIGH. The asparagus should remain crisp. Mix the soy sauce and sesame oil. Drain the asparagus well and toss with the soy sauce mixture. Sprinkle over the sesame seeds and serve hot or cold.

Ginger Broccoli

PREPARATION TIME: 20 minutes

MICROWAVE COOKING TIME: 7-8 minutes

SERVES: 4 people

675g/1½ lbs broccoli
30ml/2 tbsps oil
7.5cm/3 inch piece fresh ginger root, peeled and very finely shredded
Pinch salt
Pinch sugar
5ml/1 tsp cornflour/cornstarch
120ml/4 fl oz/½ cup light stock
Dash light soy sauce

Heat a browning dish for 5 minutes on HIGH. Cut off the tough ends of

DESSERTS

Velvet Cream

PREPARATION TIME: 10 minutes

MICROWAVE COOKING TIME:
8-9 minutes

SERVES: 4 people

570ml/1 pint/2 cups milk
60ml/4 tbsps smooth peanut butter
60g/2oz/¼ cup sugar
30ml/2 tbsps cornflour/cornstarch
60g/2oz/½ cup finely chopped, roasted
  peanuts
15ml/1 tbsp sesame seeds

Combine all but 60ml/4 tbsps of the milk with the peanut butter and sugar. Heat for 5 minutes on HIGH. Combine the remaining milk with the cornflour/cornstarch and stir into the peanut butter mixture gradually. Return to the oven and cook on HIGH for 3-4 minutes, or until the consistency of thick cream. Cook until the cornflour/cornstarch thickens completely. Serve warm or cold, topped with peanuts and sesame seeds.

Treasure Rice

PREPARATION TIME: 25 minutes

MICROWAVE COOKING TIME:
40-41 minutes

SERVES: 4-6 people

225g/8oz/3 cups glutinous rice or
  pudding/short grain rice
870ml/1½ pints/3 cups water
5ml/1 tsp salt
225g/8oz/1 cup sugar
150g/5oz/1 cup sweetened red bean
  paste

15ml/1 tbsp candied lotus seeds (optional)
30g/1oz/¼ cup blanched whole almonds
4 red glacé/candied cherries
4 green glacé/candied cherries
2 rings glacé/candied pineapple
2-3 dates, stoned
4 glacé/candied apricots

Combine rice, salt and water and cook on HIGH for 10 minutes. Add the sugar and lower the setting to LOW/DEFROST and cook for 20 minutes. Spoon half of the cooked rice into a microproof glass serving dish. Spread over the bean paste and cover with the remaining rice. Cut the fruit into pieces and arrange decoratively on top of the rice. Cover the bowl with pierced plastic wrap/cling film and cook on

MEDIUM for 4-5 minutes. If desired, combine 280ml/½ pint/1 cup water with 120g/4oz/½ cup sugar and 5ml/ 1 tsp cornflour/cornstarch in a glass measure. Cook for 6 minutes on HIGH and add a few drops almond essence/extract. Pour several spoonfuls of the sauce over the pudding and serve the rest separately.

Jade Pieces

PREPARATION TIME: 1 hour

MICROWAVE COOKING TIME: 43-49 minutes

MAKES: 24 pieces (approx.)

450g/1 lb green split peas, soaked overnight, or brought to the boil, cooked 10 minutes on HIGH and left to stand for 1 hour
120g/4oz/½ cup sugar
850ml/1½ pints/3 cups water
60ml/4 tbsps cornflour/cornstarch
1 piece preserved ginger, finely chopped
45ml/3 tbsps desiccated coconut
Few drops green food colouring

Drain the peas and return them to a large glass bowl. Add the water, loosely cover the bowl and cook on HIGH for 40-45 minutes, or until the peas are very soft. Pureé the peas with the sugar and food colouring. Mix the cornflour/cornstarch with a little water and add to the peas. Return to the bowl and cook, uncovered, 3-4 minutes until cornflour/cornstarch thickens. Add the ginger and pour into a shallow dish to the depth of 2.5cm/1 inch. Sprinkle the coconut over the surface and chill until firm. Cut into diamond shapes to serve.

Facing page: Velvet Cream (top) and Treasure Rice (bottom). This page: Date and Red Bean Winter Pudding (top) and Jade Pieces (bottom).

Date and Red Bean Winter Pudding

PREPARATION TIME: 20 minutes

MICROWAVE COOKING TIME: 17-22 minutes plus 3 minutes standing time

SERVES: 4 people

450g/1lb dried, stoned dates
850ml/1½ pints/3 cups water
180g/6oz/1½ cups red bean paste
225g/½lb/1 cup sugar
60ml/4 tbsps cornflour/cornstarch
90g/3oz/⅓ cup white vegetable shortening or margarine
Pinch salt
2.5ml/½ tsp almond essence/extract
30ml/2 tbsps flaked/sliced almonds

Place the dates in a large bowl and add the water. Cover loosely and cook 12-16 minutes on HIGH, or until the water boils and the dates begin to soften. Leave to stand 3 minutes. Drain the water from the dates and reserve 570ml/1 pint/ 2 cups of the liquid and mix with the cornflour/cornstarch, and cook 3-4 minutes on HIGH to thicken. Combine the dates, sugar, bean paste, shortening or margarine, salt and almond essence/extract in a food processor and pureé until smooth. Mix into the thickened date liquid and cook for 2 minutes on HIGH, stirring frequently. Pour into a serving bowl and chill. Sprinkle with almonds. May be served with cream if desired.

INDEX